DIFFERENTIATING INSTRUCTION

Matching Strategies with Objectives

Marie Menna Pagliaro

ROWMAN & LITTLEFIELD EDUCATION
A division of

ROWMAN & LITTLEFIELD PUBLISHERS, INC.
Lanham • New York • Toronto • Plymouth, UK

Published by Rowman & Littlefield Education
A division of Rowman & Littlefield Publishers, Inc.
A wholly owned subsidiary of The Rowman & Littlefield Publishing Group, Inc.
4501 Forbes Boulevard, Suite 200, Lanham, Maryland 20706
http://www.rowmaneducation.com

Estover Road, Plymouth PL6 7PY, United Kingdom

Copyright © 2011 by Marie Menna Pagliaro

All rights reserved. No part of this book may be reproduced in any form or by any electronic or mechanical means, including information storage and retrieval systems, without written permission from the publisher, except by a reviewer who may quote passages in a review.

British Library Cataloguing in Publication Information Available

Library of Congress Cataloging-in-Publication Data
Pagliaro, Marie Menna, 1934-
 Differentiating instruction : matching strategies with objectives / Marie Menna Pagliaro.
  p. cm.
 Includes bibliographical references.
 ISBN 978-1-61048-459-6 (cloth : alk. paper) -- ISBN 978-1-61048-460-2 (pbk. : alk. paper) -- ISBN 978-1-61048-461-9 (ebook)
 1. Individualized instruction. 2. Inclusive education. 3. Multicultural education. 4. Mainstreaming in education. I. Title.
 LB1031.P33 2011
 371.9'0460973--dc22   2011015769

∞™ The paper used in this publication meets the minimum requirements of American National Standard for Information Sciences—Permanence of Paper for Printed Library Materials, ANSI/NISO Z39.48-1992. Printed in the United States of America

CONTENTS

Introduction   v

PART I   HOW TO ACQUIRE TEACHING STRATEGIES AND IMPROVE YOUR PERFORMANCE

1   Implementing Teaching Strategies   3

PART II   TEACHER-CENTERED STRATEGIES

2   Concept Attainment   17

3   Concept Formation   25

4   The Advance Organizer   29

5   Direct Instruction   33

6   Modeling   39

7   The Lecture   43

PART III   STUDENT-CENTERED STRATEGIES

8   Problem-Based Learning   51

9	Cooperative Learning	59
10	Mastery Learning	65
11	Learning Activity Centers (Learning Stations)	71

References 77

About the Author 85

INTRODUCTION

It has been reported that most teachers, even those selected by principals to be mentor teachers—those responsible for developing new teachers—have a limited instructional repertoire, relying on only one strategy, thus preventing students from learning (Joyce & Showers, 2002). This book will help you improve the instructional strategies you are currently using and learn new ones to add to your repertoire. This variety will help you better match different kinds of objectives with corresponding instruction, so that you can deal more successfully with the diverse needs of students in your class.

Possessing a strong range of instructional strategies will also give you the flexibility to make your classes more interesting and brain compatible. Because having a number of different strategies will keep your students more meaningfully engaged in the instructional process, student misbehavior will tend to decrease, thereby minimizing your stress level.

To understand the importance of learning different strategies, Robert Marzano (2002) used the analogy of graduating successfully from navy pilot school. When the trainee enters, he or she is handed a curriculum of 22 advanced tactical strategy skills to be mastered, each with a six-point rubric. When these 22 skills are mastered, the pilot must go up against another pilot using any of the skills learned. He or she may use any of the strategies. The only condition is that the pilot must win.

Transferring this analogy to teaching, a teacher should master many strategies. It is not necessary to use all of them, but what is important is that the teacher uses the strategy that is appropriate at the time so that the student will learn.

This book is presented in three parts. You might be generally familiar with many of the strategies offered in this book, but Part I describes an innovative process that will enable you to improve your performance when implementing those strategies. You will also be able to acquire new strategies. This process involves the use of coaching rubrics, field-tested tools designed to acquire skills and develop performance step by step. A thorough explanation of their use is explained in the first chapter.

Part II focuses on teacher-directed strategies—those in which the teacher has control of the content and implements the subject matter, generally through large-class instruction. Part III concentrates on student-centered strategies—those in which students have more input and control over their learning. A summary is provided at the end of each section. After Parts II and III, a chart reviews when to use the strategies offered.

By reading this book you will understand the theory that explains why the strategies presented should work. You will learn how to apply the strategies using the coaching rubrics. How well you learn to implement the strategy depends on the amount of practice time you invest. As you review each strategy, you will begin to identify for whom it would be most applicable, what objectives could be best taught using the strategy, and when the strategy would be appropriate.

All of the strategies are based on original works. However, their implementation also includes their expansion and interpretation by subsequent researchers. Examples of strategy applications are provided from elementary through high school.

It is also noteworthy for you to understand from the beginning that teacher-centered and student-centered strategies are not mutually exclusive. Teacher-centered strategies may be used to work with students individually and in small groups. Elements of student-centered strategies may also be used with the whole class. Both the teacher-centered and student-centered strategies presented in this book keep the student involved in learning.

As you grow in your ability to deliver many different types of instruction, you will notice a significant gain in your students' achievement and fewer discipline problems. These accomplishments will generate in you a higher level of professional satisfaction. Congratulations on your performance.

Marie Menna Pagliaro

I

HOW TO ACQUIRE TEACHING STRATEGIES AND IMPROVE YOUR PERFORMANCE

IMPLEMENTING TEACHING STRATEGIES

The following chapters review many different teaching strategies. However, it is one thing to read and know about effective teaching strategies and another to actually be able to implement them.

> Whoever acquires knowledge but does not practice it is as one who ploughs but does not sow.
>
> —Saadi

Knowledge of teaching strategies reaches its full potential when you can translate that knowledge into performance.

A FRAMEWORK FOR ACQUIRING TEACHING SKILLS (STRATEGIES)

Learning even the most basic skills takes time, and developing teaching skills is a lifelong endeavor. A framework for acquiring teaching skills was offered by Joyce and Showers (1995, 2002). This framework includes: theory exploration, demonstration, practice with accompanying feedback, and adaptation and generalization.

1. *Theory exploration.* As a professional, the teacher must first understand the research, theory, and reasoning behind the skills or strategies to be learned or improved and the guiding principles that oversee their use. Study each of the remaining chapters to gain knowledge for each strategy. You can further explore teaching strategies through additional readings and by discussing the material with colleagues.
2. *Demonstration.* In this phase, the strategy to be improved or the new strategy is modeled for the teacher. Examples of the skill in action may be conducted through a live demonstration by a peer, an outside expert, through videotapes, or computer simulations. Teachers have often complained that in their teacher education programs, professors didn't model the practices that were promoted (Reiman & Thies-Sprinthall, 1998).
3. *Practice with accompanying feedback.* It has often been said that the three most important things in real estate are location, location, and location. It can also be said that the three most important activities in developing teaching strategies are practice, practice, and practice. The role of practicing cannot be overemphasized. Practice is required to develop any skill whether in the arts, sports, or teaching. Though you can practice and evaluate your own performance, practice is more effective when it occurs with colleagues. Teaching used to be a very lonely profession. When a teacher closed his door, he had to fend for himself with no input from colleagues, only an occasional observation and checklist evaluation from a supervisor or principal.

On the occasion of his retirement, John (Jack) Welch (2000), former CEO of General Electric, communicated to his employees that whatever they can do well on their own, they can do much smarter with others. Teachers are now working much smarter by diagnosing students together; planning together; co-designing and selecting assessment tools and curriculum materials; observing each other; and giving one another feedback regarding performance. Peer interaction has been demonstrated as being necessary for teacher growth (Danielson, 1996, 2007).

As soon as possible after the practice session, you should receive feedback regarding your performance from your colleagues.

Immediate feedback allows you to become aware of parts of your performance that were successful, and those that needed adjustment. Receiving this feedback prevents poor performance from becoming routine.

The strategies presented in this book involve both pre-structuring/pre-planning on your part, as well as interaction with students. When this interaction occurs within a class period, microteaching, teaching the new strategy to a small group of your students, should be used.

It is essential that the microteaching session be documented as a video or audio recording. Documentation of both the pre-structuring and interaction is of particular consequence because it has been reported historically that there is a gap in perception between what teachers think they do in the classroom and what they actually do (Good & Brophy, 1974; Hook & Rosenshine, 1979; Sadker & Sadker, 1994; Delpit, 1995).

Documentation will help you and your colleagues determine which of the steps of the strategy you implemented and which you did not. Subsequent practice and/or microteaching sessions can verify the inclusion of the steps that might have been omitted in prior sessions. Practice can then continue until the desired level of strategy acquisition has been realized.

4. *Adaptation and generalization.* There is no point in developing teaching strategies or any other classroom skills if they are not actually carried out in the classroom. Once the skills that can be implemented within a class period have been practiced with a small group of your students, the skills can then be used with the whole class.

Video recording interaction with students remains a necessity so that you can receive feedback for yourself and from your mentors/colleagues. In all cases, it is essential that you self-evaluate and self-reflect. Keep in mind that teacher self-reflection is one of the criteria for developing all teaching skills (Hanson, 1998).

Using the Power of Coaching Rubrics

To assist you in self-reflection as you endeavor to acquire and improve your knowledge and implementation of the teaching strategies covered in this book, you will be provided at appropriate intervals with personal guided observation instruments—coaching rubrics. A coaching rubric is a set of criteria to *develop* performance. Coaching rubrics do exactly what their name implies by coaching and guiding your presentation step-by-step. These rubrics also summarize the content for each strategy and document your growth, ensuring that you plan and implement the strategies successfully.

Besides all the advantages mentioned previously, coaching rubrics expose teachers to mastery performance (best practices in implementing a strategy) and offer a medium with which to:

- internalize mastery performance of that strategy
- constantly remind teachers of mastery performance
- analyze present teaching strategy performance
- compare present performance to best practices by identifying strategy steps yet to be implemented
- serve as tools for acquiring new repertoires of strategies
- foster communication and dialog among colleagues to continually identify strategy criteria
- provide a forum for discussing with colleagues more effective examples of criteria
- provide a structure for adjusting criteria and for creating new rubrics when a new strategy and/or new research emerges
- evaluate implementation of the strategy after practice

The coaching rubrics offered will empower you to take control over your own development immediately.

Teachers often have a pre-determined mindset when it comes to rubrics by thinking of them as only scoring rubrics. However, coaching rubrics are different from scoring rubrics, which are a set of criteria for *judging* performance. In a scoring rubric, the criteria (descriptors) are arranged in a hierarchy that ranges from the poorest to the best performance. A scoring rubric is holistic in that performance is either scored numerically (1–6) or verbally (such as "emerging" to "outstanding") according to a set of criteria (descriptors).

Holistic rubrics assess overall quality of student work, such as organization of a report, creativity in writing, or critical thinking. For a score to be assigned, all criteria (descriptors) have to be taken into account simultaneously (Brookhart, 2004).

Example: In a scoring rubric for map legends, box 1.1, the scores (1, 2, or 3) represent the corresponding performance levels.

Box 1.1 Map Legend Scoring Rubric

Level 3 (Higher Order): creates an original legend to communicate spatial arrangements and directions
Level 2 (Complex): interprets map subtleties that go beyond just reading the legend
Level 1 (Basic): states literal meanings of legend items (Adapted from Lazear [1998, p. 56])

You will observe in the above scoring rubric that performance levels are ranked and all levels of performance have to be considered before judging which score (1, 2, or 3) to assign.

In contrast, the criteria in coaching rubrics are not necessarily arranged in a hierarchy. Coaching rubrics are analytic in that each criterion (descriptor) assesses specific aspects of performance and is evaluated separately not by rating the criterion but by identifying specific and detailed examples of the criterion.

The criteria must also be specific and observable enough that more than one person observing the performance will be able to agree if each criterion had been demonstrated. Specificity and observability give the rubric reliability (Wiggins, 2005).

Coaching rubrics are easy to complete. After experience with the first coaching rubric, teachers have often expressed how simple these rubrics

Table 1.1 Rubrics

Scoring	Coaching
Judge performance	Develop performance
Criteria arranged in a hierarchy (performance levels)	Criteria not necessarily arranged in a hierarchy
All criteria evaluated together to assign a score (holistic)	Each criterion evaluated separately (analytic)
Score (usually numerical) assigned	Specific and accurate examples of criteria must be indicated

Table 1.2 Coaching Rubric for Professional Development (T)

Criteria (Descriptors)	Performance Indicators (Examples)
The teacher	
• identified reading for personal and professional broadening	• identified *Classroom Instruction That Works* by Robert Marzano et al.
• read the materials and was able to describe what was learned	• read text, learned that the nine major instructional strategies that affect student achievement are: identifying similarities and differences; summarized; reinforced effort; homework and practice; used non-linguistic representations, cooperative learning; set objectives; generated and tested hypotheses; used questions, cues, and advance organizers.
• used the new learning acquired from the materials in the classroom	• used similarities and differences when teaching verbs by comparing them with other verbs and contrasting them with other parts of speech
• evaluated the effect of the new learning on instruction	• evaluated students on subsequent test on which they performed significantly better than they had before I made the comparisons/contrasts and just gave them definitions and examples
• identified a relevant professional association (or associations)	• identified the ASCD
• joined the professional association(s)	• joined the ASCD in June
• participated in the association's activities and can describe what was learned	
• transferred the new learning acquired from the professional association to the classroom and evaluated the effect of the new learning	
• identified a mentor to assist in professional development	• identified veteran master teacher Marian Floyd
• identified others with whom to network	• identified and contacted June Larson and Roy Pinzer from neighboring districts
• identified ways to act as an agent to arrange for complementing my teaching	
• collaborated with colleagues to obtain feedback for self-reflection	• collaborated with fellow 4th grade teachers Lisa, Tom, and Frank
• used guided observation for self-reflection	• used the Coaching Rubric for Lesson Planning and Implementation with my colleagues to evaluate my videotape
• sought input from learners	• sought input from class every Friday in both writing and in classroom discussion regarding how well the week went and what could be done to improve instruction on the part of both the students and myself

• used a self-reflective journal	• used a self-reflective journal to jot down what happened each day. Arranged with Marian Floyd to discuss my journal once a week.
• developed a portfolio for self-reflection	
• As a result of the previous steps, identified own professional development needs	
• devised a plan to meet the needs	
• If learning/perfecting a particular skill/model was identified as a need for development, explained the theory supporting the skill/model	
• If necessary, arranged to have the skill/model demonstrated by an expert or video simulation	
• practiced the skill/model with feedback (under microteaching conditions where applicable) until a desired level of achievement was attained	
• implemented that skill/model in the classroom with the whole class	
• evaluated the implementation of that skill/model in the classroom with the whole class	

actually are to work with and how effective they actually are in improving professional practice.

As an illustration, consider The Coaching Rubric for Professional Development in table 1.2. The criteria for this rubric were developed by a group of teachers after studying effective practices in professional development. The rubric is partially filled in to explain how to use the remaining rubrics in this book. Before you continue reading, examine this sample rubric carefully. Viewing the rubric will provide you with a frame of reference and a context for the explanation that follows.

You will notice that the coaching rubric in table 1.2 is divided into two columns—Criteria (Descriptors) and Performance Indicators (Examples), and that some of the Performance Indicators are completed and others are blank. The column on the left lists specific research-based skills (criteria) associated with a particular rubric.

Coaching rubrics represent mastery performance. When working with coaching rubrics, you should understand from the beginning that it is not expected, necessary, or in many cases possible for anyone can perform all of the criteria in the rubric all the time (Wiggins, 1998). However, because the criteria are determined to be integral to implementing the strategy, employing most of the criteria will increase the chances for reaching all learners successfully.

As already indicated, depending on the outcome, criteria in a coaching rubric are not necessarily listed in order. For instance, you can join a professional organization before identifying reading for personal broadening. You can identify peers with whom to work before doing either.

The column on the right of table 1.2 presents the Performance Indicators. The teacher (colleagues/evaluators) must put in writing in this column exactly how each criterion was actually demonstrated, providing specific, detailed, and appropriate examples. This process provides objective and more reliable performance data, making it easier for several observers (peers/colleagues) to agree that the performance has actually occurred.

Documentation of the examples is more focused and precise because the same verb and tense combination stated in the criterion is also used in the indicator. Verbs used in the Criteria (Descriptors) are expressed in the past tense, describing what the teacher actually did, not what she plans to do.

For instance, the third criterion in the Coaching Rubric for Professional Development is, "Enlisted peers with whom to collaborate." Inappropriate ways to state the Performance Indicator would be stating what will be done in that category; putting a check, writing "Satisfied," "Completed," "Yes," or an equivalent term next to the corresponding criterion; numerically scoring the criterion; or offering an irrelevant example.

Appropriate ways of stating the Performance Indicator for the above would be writing the names of the persons who agreed to be collaborators next to the corresponding criterion, such as "Enlisted (same verb and tense stated in the criterion) Paul and Sally from my teaching team." Otherwise, the Performance Indicator for this criterion would remain blank.

Because the documentation is so specific, coaching rubrics are more informative than the traditional type of rubric that judges performance through rating scales where raters place a check mark for each criterion in the corresponding box.

Traditional rubrics, with scale variations (1–4, 1–5, 1–7), are commonly used to evaluate teachers. However, these rubrics "don't give specific enough information . . . to use for further learning" (Brookhart, 2004, p. 77). Receiving a reported rating (score), such as 3 for Average on any scale used, while it does give some feedback, does not inform the teacher during the self-reflective process what "Average" performance actually is nor guide her how to improve in that category.

You have already observed that there are blank spaces under Performance Indicators in the Coaching Rubric for Professional Development. Spaces that are not filled provide specific feedback identifying where performance was not implemented. In these cases, subsequent practice would aim at trying to include these criteria.

The first session using any rubric obtains baseline data regarding performance on that rubric. From the baseline data, it can then be determined which additional criteria (descriptors) should be demonstrated in future performance. After obtaining the baseline data, the teacher can then practice, addressing the implementation of only a few criteria at one time.

In their attempt to offer a teacher evaluation system that goes beyond using observation forms and changing them periodically, Danielson & McGreal (2000) have offered a blueprint with three essential attributes: the "what," the "how," and "trained evaluators." The "what" includes clear criteria for exemplary practice based on current research; the "how" involves the ability of school districts to guarantee that teachers can demonstrate the criteria; and "trained evaluators" are those who can assure that, regardless of who is conducting the evaluation, the judgment is consistent and reliable.

Coaching rubrics fulfill all three criteria suggested by Danielson & McGreal (2000). These rubrics express criteria for mastery performance (exemplary practice); help teachers demonstrate criteria by indicating which have not been evidenced by appropriate examples, thereby identifying areas (criteria) needed for implementation; and provide a forum for "reliable evaluations" in which the teacher must indicate and peer evaluators must agree which specific and accurate examples of criteria were fulfilled during actual performance.

Table 1.3 Completing Performance Indicators for Corresponding Coaching Rubric Criteria

Correct Completion	Incorrect Completion
Use the same verb	Use a different verb
Use the same tense	Write what will be done
Provide a specific detailed example	Provide a general or vague example
Provide a relevant example	Provide an irrelevant example
	Use terms such as "Yes," "Completed," or "Satisfied," place a check mark or score numerically

Moreover, in the discussions of the examples among all participants, suggestions can be offered for more effective examples that the teacher could have implemented. This interaction is professionalism at its best because it is highly successful in improving instruction and growth for all participants (Danielson, 2007).

Using the coaching rubrics, you are now prepared to apply the framework for acquiring teaching skills (Joyce & Showers, 1995, 2002) introduced earlier in this chapter: theory exploration, demonstration, practice with feedback, and adaptation and generalization. You should understand why the criteria in the coaching rubric are essential (*theory exploration*).

Familiarity with the research and discussion with peers are crucial processes in assisting participants in both identifying and then internalizing the criteria. If a question about any criterion is not clear, an example of the criterion should be provided (*demonstration*). Practicing the criteria using the coaching rubric can then follow in a controlled environment.

You may recall the old adage that practice makes perfect. Wolfe (2001) reminded teachers that practice also makes permanent. And Vince Lombardi taught his football players that perfect practice makes permanent. These are the reasons that you must practice correctly with complete understanding of the rubric criteria and why they are important.

Both you and your colleagues should evaluate your performance on the rubric thus far (*practice with accompanying feedback*). If you and your colleagues are satisfied with your performance, you can then implement the new strategy with your entire class (*adaptation and generalization*).

Some coaching rubrics, such as Concept Attainment, have criteria that can be demonstrated within a class period. Other coaching rubrics, such as Cooperative Learning, Problem Solving, and the Professional Development rubric provided above as an illustration, take a longer time to implement. Coaching rubrics that take a longer time to implement are coded (T).

Above all, it must be clear that coaching rubrics are *dynamic*. These living documents are works in progress, guidelines whose criteria should be modified when new research develops. As more studies reveal different criteria for performance excellence and as new and validated strategies and criteria are proposed, collaborators should revise rubrics and/or develop new ones.

Also, it is essential to understand that a teacher can demonstrate all the criteria in the rubric and yet be ineffective. The reason is that teaching is more than the sum of its parts. There are always intangibles involved that can contribute to effective or ineffective performance (box 1.2).

Box 1.2 Directions for Using Coaching Rubrics

1. Identify collaborators (colleagues) and ensure that you and your colleagues fully understand and agree with the rubric criteria (descriptors).
2. Rubrics that take time (T) should be checked periodically to determine progress. When performance involves interacting with students that can be completed within a class period, audiotape or videotape the delivery.
3. As soon as possible after the performance, document it with colleagues by writing next to each criterion under the Performance Indicators column a specific and relevant example where you demonstrated any of the criteria. Write the indicator using the same verb and same tense stated in the criterion.
4. Identify no more than three additional criteria. Concentrate on only those criteria in subsequent performance using microteaching with audiotaping or videotaping when appropriate.
5. Continue identifying additional criteria to be demonstrated in your performance and documenting that performance until a mutually agreed upon level of achievement is reached.

PART I SUMMARY

Knowledge of teaching strategies (skills) is useless unless this knowledge can be translated into performance. Teaching strategies (skills) can be implemented by understanding the theory behind them, having the strategies demonstrated, practicing the strategies with feedback, and transferring them to the classroom. As with all other skills, teaching skills take time and practice to develop.

To acquire any teaching strategy, practicing that strategy with documentation is necessary. Practice is more effective when it occurs collaboratively, with colleagues' feedback as well as with self-feedback.

Coaching rubrics are guided observation instruments that assist teachers in acquiring, developing, and evaluating teaching skills. Coaching rubrics are divided into criteria and performance indicators. The performance indicators must be completed using a specific and relevant example of the corresponding criterion using the same verb and tense as that stated in the criterion. When no specific example of the criterion has been demonstrated, the performance indicator remains blank.

II

TEACHER-DIRECTED STRATEGIES

2

CONCEPT ATTAINMENT

THEORY

A *concept* can be defined in several different ways. For the purposes of this chapter, a concept is defined as a category that groups similar objects, people, or events. Concepts allow us to categorize objects and then recognize members of that category (Gagne et al., 1993). *Dog* is a category that includes poodles, terriers, chihuahuas, collies, and other pure breeds, as well as mixed breeds. Categories allow us to organize an enormous amount of data into manageable segments.

Concepts are the foundation of our thinking and our communicating. We need concepts to learn principles (generalizations, laws, rules) that express the relationship between two or more concepts.

Example: One of Newton's laws is, "Every action has an equal and opposite reaction."

To understand this law, a student must first understand its foundational concepts—action, equal, opposite, and reaction.

In turn, principles are needed to solve problems. The principle (law) can be applied to the problem of getting a rocket off the ground and maintaining its travel through space.

To summarize, concepts are needed to form principles (generalization, laws, rules) and principles are needed to solve problems. It is of prime importance that your students learn concepts well because once misconceptions occur, they are very difficult to change.

Most of the groundwork for concept attainment was laid by Bruner, Goodnow, and Austin (1967). Implementation of the concept attainment strategy has been and continues to be developed and refined by Joyce et al. (2004).

The members of a category or class are grouped together by certain attributes or distinguishing features. The attributes may be crucial or noncrucial. A chair always has a seat, legs (usually four), and a back support. These are its crucial attributes. A chair can also be high, low, wide, narrow, made of metal, wood, plastic, and embellished in different ways. These are its noncrucial attributes.

All categories do not have clear-cut defining attributes (Benjafield, 1992). Though flying is common to most birds, it is not a crucial attribute of its class. If it were, the nonflying penguin or ostrich would not be considered birds. A house is not always a place where people live. It could be the House of Representatives, a house of ill repute, or a restaurant with a specialty, such as House of Burgers.

Because concepts are abstractions, the only way they can be dealt with is through examples (exemplars), those which belong in the category, and nonexamples (nonexemplars), those which do not belong in the category. However, you recall from the previous paragraph that category membership can be unclear. Schwartz & Reisberg (1991) referred to these unclear categories as those that have graded membership. Some objects, events, or people provide better examples of the concept or category than those which have graded membership.

Implementation

When applying concept attainment in the classroom, the teacher must first establish the objective she wishes to teach (learning the concept in this case) by informing the students that she has an idea in her mind she wants them to guess. The teacher presents several matched pairs that contain examples of the idea and nonexamples of the idea.

Examples are displayed in the Example column, and nonexamples are displayed in the Nonexample column. The students are to identify the characteristics or attributes of the examples by comparing the examples and contrasting them with the nonexamples. The question the students are to consider is, "What do the examples have that the nonexamples do not have?"

When presenting the set of examples, the teacher should use the best representatives of the category, known as *prototypes* (Rosch, 1973). In order to have students concentrate on the crucial attributes of the best set of examples (prototypes), it is essential that the prototypes have as different as possible noncrucial attributes.

For instance, in the case of teaching the concept triangles, the teacher should present triangle examples of different sizes, side lengths, and colors so that the students will concentrate on the crucial attribute—a closed figure with three sides.

When presenting the set of example and nonexample pairs, the teacher should make each pair's noncrucial attributes as similar as possible so that the students can concentrate on the differences between examples and nonexamples. In the case of teaching the concept of two-syllable words, the teacher can use "strangle" as an example and "string" as a nonexample. Because both words start with the same consonant blend (st), the students can then examine more efficiently the differences between them.

Look at the following word pairs to see how the noncrucial attributes of the examples (words that contain silent letters) are different from each other (in initial letters, number of syllables, parts of speech) and how the example and nonexample pairs are similar.

Examples	**Nonexamples**
salmon	salad
castle	caddy
almond	altar
gnat	not
sword	swing
knowingly	factual
whole	hole

Example and nonexample sets can be introduced as a single pair first or all together. Examine the list of examples and nonexamples for teaching the concept of prime numbers.

Attributes	Examples	Nonexamples
	7	8
	2	20
	5	4
	11	9

If the teacher introduced just the first pair, 7 and 8, the students might decide (hypothesize) that the attribute "odd number" is possessed by the example and not by the nonexample. The teacher would write "odd number" under the Attributes list even though it is not the correct attribute of prime numbers.

At this stage in the lesson, the students' guess would be correct. Because 7 and 8 are both single-digit numerals, and, therefore, similar in this respect, the students would not tend to offer "single digit" as an attribute of the example 7.

In the next matched pair, 2 and 20, the attribute, odd number, would be eliminated because 2 is even. The students would now have to decide what 7 and 2, both examples, have in common that is still different from 8 and 20, the nonexamples. If the students hypothesize that 7 and 2 are "less than" 8 and 20, the next pair the teacher introduces, 5 and 4 would eliminate the attribute "less than." The students would continue comparing the examples and contrasting them with the nonexamples.

The pair 11 and 9 represents the first time a two-digit numeral is offered as an example, and an odd number, a nonexample. This pair further assists in the comparing and contrasting. Eventually, the students should determine that the numbers represented by the examples have only themselves and one as factors. They have guessed the teacher's idea—that some numbers are only divisible by themselves and one (attribute of the concept). The students can then be told that these numbers are called *prime numbers* (the label).

If a student offered the actual concept, prime numbers, as an attribute, the teacher would have to ask for the attribute(s) of prime numbers. If the student cannot identify its attributes, he does not know the concept. Eventually, the students can be told that 1 is a special number that is a factor of all numbers. It is a special number called the *unit* that is neither prime nor composite, a number that has other factors besides itself and one.

Many suggestions by the students might be unanticipated, and the teacher, even if she plans the matched pairs carefully, must be armed with or think "on the spot" of additional examples and nonexample pairs which will finally elicit the crucial attributes of any concept she wishes to teach.

The same examples offered can be presented all at the same time instead of one by one. The students would then compare all the examples and contrast them with the nonexamples to come up with the attribute(s). The teacher might still need to offer additional example and nonexample pairs.

Once the essential attributes of a concept are identified, the students basically know the concept. This is true whether or not they have a label (name) for the concept. The name or label is less important than knowing the attributes. However, eventually the set of attributes has to be labeled.

Remember that knowing the label is not necessarily the same as knowing the concept. Students will often use labels for concepts without having a clear idea of their attributes. A typical example is a kindergarten student who can verbally say "six" but cannot count six objects if they are positioned differently. The same student might also count the same object more than once or skip the object.

Adults often use terms they do not fully understand. Most adults thought that the term "impeach" meant that a president could be thrown out of office instead of that the president would undergo a trial to see if he should be removed.

When a student uses a term and you are not sure whether or not she really understands it, ask for an example. Also ask for a nonexample because in order to understand a concept, a student should know what it is as well as what it is not.

The teacher further determines whether the students know the concept by offering one at a time in random order different examples and nonexamples that the students have to place under the correct column. Students must state why they have made their placement choice.

The next step is having the students offer their own examples and nonexamples and also list them in the proper columns. At this time, the students should be able to explain or justify why their offerings are examples or not. In the final step, the teacher has the student apply the concept to deepen understanding. Students may identify prime numbers in their textbooks, anywhere else in the environment, or use prime numbers to do prime factorization.

It is more effective to present nonexamples that do not all belong to the same category. This was unavoidable in the prime number example where all the nonexamples had to be composite numbers. However, if "adjective" is the concept to be taught, the teacher should display nonexamples that represent various other parts of speech, such as verbs, adverbs, conjunctions, pronouns, adverbs, prepositions, or interjections. Using nonexamples from different categories makes it easier to contrast the examples and nonexamples so that the crucial attributes of the examples stand out.

Examples and nonexamples can take many different forms. They can be sentences.

Examples	**Nonexamples**
Walking is good for you.	You are *walking* too fast
I like *walking*.	The boys, *walking* and tripping along the way, were exhausted.
With *walking*, you get good exercise.	While he was *walking*, he tripped on a rock.
My mother's favorite activity is *walking*.	Let the *walking* boys take a rest.

Highlighting in some way the word *walking* allows the student to concentrate on the use of that particular word in the sentences. Given enough examples and nonexamples, the student should be able to recognize that in the examples, walking is the –ing form of a verb that is used as a noun, not as a participle (assuming the student knows before the lesson what a participle is). The concept the teacher has in mind is *gerund*.

Examples and nonexamples can be symbols or pictures. If the attributes of Impressionist paintings were to be identified, all the examples would be paintings from that period, and the nonexamples would be paintings from several other periods.

CONCEPT ATTAINMENT

Table 2.1 Coaching Rubric for Concept Attainment

Criteria (Descriptors)	Performance Indicators (Examples)
The teacher • determined whether students were experientially ready for the new concept • informed students that he had an idea (concept) they were to guess • informed students that examples and non-examples of the concept would be presented and the students were to identify the attributes (distinguishing features) of the concept by comparing examples and contrasting the examples with non-examples • presented and displayed an initial positive example (prototype) that clearly contained all the essential attributes of the concept and wrote this example under the Example column • presented immediately afterward an initial non-example which contained none of the essential attributes of the concept and wrote this non-example under the Non-example column • requested students to contrast the example with the non-example and state what attributes the example had that the non-example did not have • listed the elicited attributes on the board under the Attributes heading • presented an additional example and non-example • asked the students to compare the examples and contrast them with the non-examples • eliminated attributes from the list that were not possessed by all the examples • provided more example and non-example pairs, and had students compare the examples and contrast them with non-examples until all essential attributes of the examples were identified and non-essential attributes were eliminated • provided in all examples non-critical attributes of the examples that were very different • provided in all example and non-example pairs, non-critical attributes that were very similar • asked the students to examine the examples to determine if the identified attributes were possessed by all of the examples	

If a student offered a category (concept) as an answer instead of attributes,
- asked the student to clarify what the category meant (give its attributes)
- presented one-by-one a random mixture of examples and non-examples, and asked students to place them in the proper column
- asked students to explain why they put the examples and non-examples in the selected column
- requested that students create their own examples and non-examples and place them in proper column
- asked students to explain why the suggestions they offered were examples or non-examples
- provided experiences for students to apply the concept

A concept attainment lesson can also be taught using an expository or direct presentation form instead of an inductive approach. Using the expository method, the teacher would begin by identifying and defining the concept. Then she would provide the crucial attributes of the concept and identify examples and nonexamples. In the final step, she would have the students offer their own examples and nonexamples.

Even though the expository approach can be effective, the inductive approach presented earlier, in which the students must discover the attributes for themselves, gets the students more actively involved mentally, and discovering is a better memory technique.

3

CONCEPT FORMATION

In the Concept Attainment model just presented, students were asked to determine the attributes of a concept already held in the teacher's mind. The students then compared examples of the concept and contrasted them with nonexamples. In the Concept Formation model, students must make a decision regarding how they will develop (form) categories from attributes.

THEORY

The concept formation model was developed by Taba (1967) in a social studies curriculum where lessons, units, and entire courses integrated thinking with content. Taba developed her strategy upon certain assumptions.

- The student can be taught to think. The teacher should assist the student in developing inductive thinking.
- Thinking results when there is a transaction between the student and data. The teacher guides students in this transaction by presenting them with data from different sources, having them orga-

nize the data, connect items in the data, then make generalizations and inferences.
- Thought processes come about in a "lawful" sequence. Skills build on already mastered skills. It is the teacher's role to ensure that prior skills are achieved before continuing with other skills. (Joyce & Weil, 2000)

Four different inductive thinking skills have been developed from Taba's model. These are concept formation, data interpretation, application of principles, and conflict resolution—along with corresponding teaching strategies for each one. In this chapter, only the first, concept formation, is covered.

As already indicated earlier in chapter 2, the development or formation of concepts is the most basic form of knowledge. Concepts are building blocks without which other cognitive processes cannot take place. Principles and generalizations depend on the relationships between or among concepts, and problem solving depends on principles and generalizations.

Implementation

Concept Formation has three parts: *data collection*—securing and enumerating data relevant to a topic being studied; *data grouping*—reorganizing the data into categories with members having the same attributes; and *group labeling*—giving a name to the categories developed. The result, according to the theory, should be the formation of major concepts from broad categories of related data.

In the first part, collecting the data, the data may be listed by the students or given by the teacher. For example, if you were asked to list the data in this book so far, you might include the following: system, teacher-directed strategy, concept, model, attribute, example, concept attainment, prototype, category, strategy, nonexample, graded membership, group, or matched pairs of examples and nonexamples.

Listing data is an important skill because it involves differentiating relevant from irrelevant information. Every student can participate in the process, regardless of ability.

In the second part, grouping the data, students classify the data and justify the classification. In the example above, students might group prototype and example together because they should both be the best representatives of a group, or they should be examples dissimilar enough that the students can focus on crucial attributes.

Students might group example, nonexample, and matched pairs of examples and nonexamples together because they help find attributes. Strategy, system, and model can be grouped because they generally mean the same thing.

The teacher guides the students in grouping the data through clear directions:

- Focus the grouping on the basis of common attributes, not labels.
- Create at least five or six groups. If this number is not specified, students, especially with their first experience with concept formation, may be apt to form one similar group and classify the rest as "other."
- Include all of the data in the grouping. No items should be left out.
- An item of data may be used in more than one group.

After all grouping is completed, the groups are displayed on the board or on posters. In this way, students share their groups with one another and can readily see that a member of one group can also hold membership in another, or others. From the original data, students may also suggest additional data items to place in groups formed by peers. Students of all abilities can participate at their own levels, with lower achievers more apt to form groups with more concrete or descriptive items and higher achievers likely to form more abstract groups.

During the third part, labeling the groups, the students must assign a phrase or word that describes what is the same about all the items in the group. "Things that are made of metal," "things that are made of metal and wood," and "breakfast foods" are examples.

After all the groups are displayed and labeled, the teacher fosters the discovery of new attributes and different relationships among the items and labels. For example, students can see that an item of data can fit into several different groups. Eventually, the students are encouraged to discover hierarchies in the relationships by determining which labels can include others and which can fit under other labels.

Concept formation is an excellent activity to employ at the end of a unit, a chapter, or after reading a story to conduct review, discover new relationships, or deepen understanding.

Table 3.1 Coaching Rubric for Concept Formation

Criteria (Descriptors)	Performance Indicators (Examples)
Data Gathering After studying a unit, topic, chapter, novel, or taking a field trip, etc., the teacher • asked students to enumerate relevant data or provided corresponding data for students If the data were provided by the students, the teacher • ensured everyone's participation in the data gathering • ensured that all students understood each item of data • elicited data without concept labeling *Data Grouping* • instructed clearly how to group data • asked students to explain their grouping • provided a means for displaying all groups *Labeling* • asked students to identify a label for the group • asked students to check that each item in the group fit the label • asked students to check the items in the group for additional attributes • asked students to check for other items in the data that may belong in the group • asked students to make associations between and among labels • identified hierarchies among labels	

4

THE ADVANCE ORGANIZER

THEORY

David Ausubel (1963) is an educational psychologist concerned with meaningful as opposed to rote learning. To understand his theory, consider the following paragraph adapted from Davis (1983).

> Pteropus is a member of the Pteropidae family of Megachiroptera. Unlike members of Microchiroptera, Pteropus eats fruit . . . roosts in trees, looks like a fox, and uses its eyes quite a bit. (p. 219)

Do you think you know what Pteropus is? Probably not. Most teachers do not know when they read the paragraph. The important consideration is why they do not know. Do you think you know why?

The reason is that there is nothing in the paragraph to associate Pteropus with what the reader already knows. If the paragraph began by stating that *chiroptera* is the scientific label for *bats*, the reader would likely have the cognitive structure (category), bats, to associate with Pteropus.

Ausubel's theory is relatively simple. "If I had to reduce all of educational psychology to just one principle, I would say this: The most important single factor influencing learning is what the learner already knows. Ascertain this and teach him accordingly" (Ausubel, Novak, &

Hanesian, 1978, p. iv). Connecting new material to ideas or categories previously learned gives meaning to the new material.

The existence of a set of categories, a cognitive structure, is the main factor that determines learning. Learning occurs when new material is included or "subsumed" into an existing cognitive structure by hooking new concepts to old ones. The teacher should be familiar with general inclusive concepts of the discipline he is teaching. These general inclusive concepts, known as *subsumers*, provide what Ausubel calls *anchorage* with which to incorporate new material.

The most general inclusive concepts are introduced to the students all at once, in advance. The inclusive concepts should be reviewed with the students, after which more specific content can be introduced. The concepts are structured in a downward hierarchy from general to specific with the broadest categories on top and the more differentiated concepts underneath (Joyce et al., 2004).

Ausubel (1997) has identified the broad inclusive concepts as advance organizers. The purpose of the advance organizer is to close the gap between what the learner already knows and what she needs to know before she can successfully learn new material. Advance organizers are familiar concepts the teacher uses to hook or anchor new information. Because the organizers go from top to bottom, they provide explaining power with which to absorb new material.

In the paragraph presented at the beginning of this section, knowing the category "bat," the advance organizer, can make it easier for a student to understand the different sizes, mega and micro, as well as distinguishing characteristics of bats of each size. Using meaningful broad concepts on which to hook new information makes the new learning more efficient, thus reducing the chances of forgetting.

Implementation

To absorb new information, there must be top-down communication with a process of progressive differentiation. In this process, the most inclusive and general ideas are presented first. Then, more detailed and specific ideas are progressively introduced. Finally, there is a process of integrative reconciliation, where new ideas are carefully related to (integrated with) prior learning.

THE ADVANCE ORGANIZER

There are two types of organizers: *expository* and *comparative*. The expository organizers are larger organizers (concepts), which include the new material, thus allowing anchorage for more detailed new material. Doctor is an expository organizer that includes physicians, Ph.Ds, dentists, chiropractors, podiatrists, or anyone else with the title "Doctor."

Comparative organizers are at the same level as that of new content. They allow the student to compare and contrast similarities and differences among concepts at that level. Physicians, dentists, Ph.Ds, chiropractors, and optometrists are comparative organizers with different functions, training, and expectations; therefore, these doctors are able to be distinguished from one another.

The advance organizer is useful when it is introduced at the beginning of a unit, a chapter, a topic, or a novel, particularly when a lot of verbal material must be learned. Once the students absorb the mind set of the general content organization, they learn where new information fits into that organization.

Figure 4.1 is an example of an advance organizer.

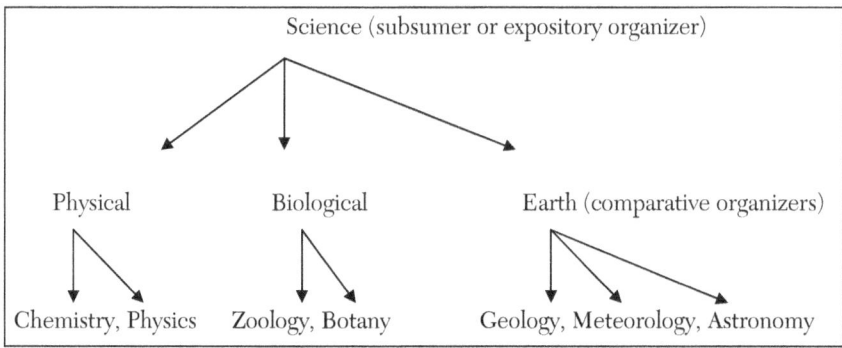

Figure 4.1 Advance Organizer for Science

The advance organizer is not the same as a semantic web or graphic organizer, which may be arranged in an order other than a hierarchy. The advance organizer is always presented in a hierarchy. Even though the organizer is deductive as opposed to inductive in nature, it still engages students by having them establish relationships between and among concepts, thus keeping students meaningfully involved in learning.

Table 4.1 Coaching Rubric for the Advance Organizer

Criteria (Descriptors)	Performance Indicators (Examples)
Planning The teacher • identified the major organizing concepts of the subject for herself • arranged subsumers in a hierarchy with the "largest" (most inclusive) on top • identified attributes of each subsumer • identified examples of each subsumer • placed expository organizers on a higher level than comparative organizers • placed comparative organizers on the same level *Presentation* The teacher • presented to students in writing the entire Advance Organizer • emphasized connections between the new material and what the students already knew • presented attributes of each subsumer • presented examples of each subsumer, compared similarities and dissimilarities between and among the subsumers • asked students to put in their own words the attributes of the subsumers • asked students to compare and contrast the attributes of the subsumers • asked students to explain the relationships in the Advance Organizer • kept the Advance Organizer displayed	

5

DIRECT INSTRUCTION

THEORY

Though strands of behavior theory, such as reinforcement, shaping (reinforcing small steps in completing a task instead of waiting for entire completion), teaching in small segments, and practice can be identified in direct instruction, there is no firm theory upon which to base this system. Instead, direct instruction evolved as a result of research regarding what teacher qualities and behaviors led to high student achievement (Rosenshine & Furst, 1971, 1973).

Eventually, Rosenshine (1979) developed ten variables that had either historically been positively correlated with student achievement or held the most promise for additional research. Rosenshine (1995) subsequently verified his research. His suggestions based on his variable are similar to the structure offered by Slavin (1994). Of the ten variables, those that consistently produced positive student achievements were:

1. businesslike and task-oriented behaviors in the classroom (a nononsense approach on the part of the teacher and the students), and
2. the amount of subject matter covered in class that is closely associated with the amount of time students are actively involved in learning the subject matter.

The term that Rosenshine coined, "academic engaged time," which embodies these two principles, forms the basis of the direct instruction model. It means directing the student's full attention to the amount of subject matter covered. The principle that the more time spent actively engaged, thus allowing more content covered, the greater the achievement was also reported by the research of McDonald (1976).

Before studying the direct instruction strategy, be forewarned that it contradicts much of what you likely learned in educational psychology and what many consider to be effective classroom practices. Some of the effective practices the Direct Instruction model contradicts are:

- emphasizing student-centered learning
- fostering higher cognitive thinking
- allowing students to choose activities
- teaching through discovery
- using simulations and games

It is noteworthy that Rosenshine (1979) found that both criticizing students and employing varieties of learning activities were correlated with lower student achievement. He also found that using varieties of learning activities produced inattention and disorder. You will recall that inattention and disorder both interfere with Rosenshine's focus on student attention and amount of content covered.

It should also be noted that in covering content, Rosenshine makes an important distinction between time assigned or allocated to a subject and time engaged, in which students are actually working on a subject. In a class where the teacher is assigned 40 minutes, out of which students are actively engaged only 25 minutes, it would be predicted that there would be less achievement than in a class where the teacher is assigned 30 minutes, out of which students are actively engaged 20 minutes.

Cangelosi (2008) makes the point that transition time, the time between tasks, should be minimized in order to maximize allocated time.

> The more allocated time you have available, the more time students have for being engaged in learning activities. Of course, making more allocated time available does not necessarily result in greater achievement unless

the learning activities are worthwhile and the additional allocated time actually results in additional engaged time (Cangelosi, 2008, p. 78).

IMPLEMENTATION

For a teacher to promote actively engaged time, an instructional framework must be followed.

1. The teacher is in control of the curriculum. He determines instructional goals. These goals are concerned with academics, not affective (personal or social) matters.
2. The teacher ensures that the goals are communicated to all students.
3. The teacher decides which academic materials are suitable for achieving the goals and which will correspond with the students' cognitive levels.
4. A broad amount of content is covered.
5. The time assigned to covering the content is adequate, with the teacher pacing the instructional activity.
6. Both content and classroom interaction are highly structured.
7. The atmosphere is positive but businesslike and academic without being authoritarian.
8. Student work is closely monitored.
9. Questions asked are those that check for understanding and are on a low level, not those that require interpretation and use up academic time.

You will note that in order to implement the above framework, certain features must be present (Joyce & Weil, 2000; Joyce et al., 2004).

- *Teacher-centered instruction.* The teacher decides the content to be taught, the learning environment, and the activities. The teacher sets high expectations for academic excellence with the corresponding behavior to achieve excellence.
- *Academic focus.* The teacher is task-oriented, determined that his students will achieve, and keeps the students focused on completing academic work. Affective matters are not discussed and the

use of nonacademic materials, such as games, arts and crafts, and puzzles, is not encouraged. Emphasis on academic focus as a determinant of student achievement was verified by Rosenshine (1985) in subsequent research.
- *Maximizing learning time.* Closely associated with academic focus is using learning time productively. The teacher keeps the students on task through structure and careful supervision.
- *Large group instruction.* Research has demonstrated that when group work is used in the classroom, academic engaged time is only about 70 percent of assigned time (Soar, 1973), whereby academic engaged time in closely supervised groups is 95 percent of assigned time (Fisher et al., 1977). Because large groups allow for greater monitoring, students can spend more time academically engaged (Rosenshine, 1979).
- *Controlled practice.* Content is introduced in segments followed by structured practice, carefully monitored guided practice in which the teacher determines how well the students have achieved the objectives. Once the teacher is secure that the students have attained the objectives, independent practice allows the students to reinforce the learning.

Direct Instruction has five phases.

1. The teacher provides an *orientation* to the lesson by informing the students of the lesson objective, explaining the content and how it is connected to prior knowledge, and discussing the overall lesson procedures, including the parts, the activities, and the students' responsibilities.
2. In the *presentation* phase, the new concept (with examples) or skill (with steps) is taught using demonstrations and illustrations both oral and, when appropriate, visual. The teacher checks for understanding by having the students recall what they have learned.
3. The teacher leads the students with *structured practice*, during which time they practice with additional examples and/or work through each step in a skill. The students usually practice as a group and write answers with the teacher using an overhead so that students can view each step. This procedure gives the teacher

feedback so that he can reinforce accurate responses and correct misconceptions.
4. Students are involved in *guided practice*, where they are able to work on their own with support from the teacher. She assesses students' work, monitors their progress, and provides corrective feedback for those who need it.
5. *Independent practice* now follows for students who have achieved an accuracy level of at least 85 percent. New learning is reinforced and fluency developed. During this phase, students practice on their own with delayed feedback. Soon afterward, the teacher reviews their work to ensure accuracy and provide corrective feedback for those who have not demonstrated an appropriate mastery level (Joyce et al., 2004).

Before completing this section on Direct Instruction, several points need to be addressed. Critics have complained about the little attention Direct Instruction provides for the affective needs of students. However, research has demonstrated that classrooms with high task orientation lead to high achievement, and high achievement is positively correlated with self-esteem (Covington & Beery, 1976).

Classes with high levels of permissiveness, where students were able to choose activities based on interest were distinguished by lower academic achievement, general disorderliness, weak writing skills, and lower self-concept (Solomon & Kendall, 1976). These researchers also suggested, however, a balance between academic and affective teaching, a notion with which Rosenshine himself agrees.

Other critics claim that Direct Instruction transmits knowledge instead of allowing students to construct it (Berg & Clough, 1991), discourages high-level thinking, and uses traditional teaching methods, casting aside more innovative approaches. Yet, Direct Instruction can be an active approach to learning, by which the teacher can promote understanding, structure the content to prevent gaps in student knowledge, and provide enough practice with guidance to ensure effective performance (Anderson et al., 1995).

Ellis (2001), in his summary of the research on Direct Instruction, stated:

It is difficult to know how to conclude a chapter devoted to a topic that has such a solid record of supportive evidence behind it but which is not particularly liked by large numbers of teachers.

Such is the case with Direct Instruction. Well, broccoli has a pretty solid record, and yet it is easy to find people who don't like and won't eat the green stuff.... Maybe Direct Instruction is the broccoli of educational practice, good for you but not everybody's favorite dish (p. 226–227).

Ellis (2001) goes on to note that in a synthesis of the research by Chall (1999), a renowned reading specialist, it was reported that traditional approaches to reading (direct instruction, phonics, and decoding) were more effective (table 5.1) as compared to more progressive approaches (whole-language, emphasis on meaning, and phonics as needed).

Table 5.1 Coaching Rubric for Direct Instruction

Criteria (Descriptors)	Performance Indicators (Examples)
The teacher • identified lesson objective (content or skill) without input from the students • connected the new objective with previous content • conveyed a high expectation that the objective would be achieved If necessary, • reminded students what corresponding behavior would be proper to achieve the lesson objective • explained the new concept or skill • presented the new material in relatively small segments • modeled the instruction by demonstrating or providing examples • checked for understanding after each segment by providing students with controlled practice all together under teacher direction • kept the activities paced • kept the atmosphere businesslike • avoided discussing affective concerns • monitored performance of all students • provided guided practice for students who were achieving the objective to continue working independently in their seats • provided further instruction and/or practice for students who needed it When confident that students were performing the objective well, • reinforced instruction through independent practice	

6

MODELING

THEORY

Initial research regarding the effects of learning through models has been conducted by Miller and Dollard (1941), Bandura and Walters (1963), and Bandura (1969, 1974). A foremost authority on the subject of modeling, Albert Bandura has demonstrated that exposure to models can produce four separate results: the *observational learning (modeling) effect*; the *inhibitory effect*; the *disinhibitory effect*; and the *response facilitation (eliciting) effect*.

Observational learning (modeling) allows a person to acquire an entirely new set of behaviors (response repertoire) by observing the performance of others. Think of how you learned how to hold eating utensils, pronounce words, develop speech patterns, respond to disappointment, or react to getting a cut on your finger. Chances are you learned how to behave through observing models, in most cases, your parents (or caretakers) or peers.

Through the inhibitory effect, inhibition or suppression of previously learned responses became strengthened. Observers who saw models punished for misbehavior tended to decrease their own misbehavior.

Through the disinhibitory effect, the inhibition or suppression of previously learned behaviors became weakened. Observers who saw models rewarded for misbehavior tended to increase their own misbehavior.

In the response facilitation (eliciting) effect, the behavior of the model influenced the observer by facilitating a response repertoire already present in the observer. The model provided discriminative cues that triggered similar responses in the observer.

Most of the research regarding modeling was focused on deviant behavior. When applied to teacher education, the application of modeling concentrated on developing observational learning, the type of learning that is the thrust of this section.

Teaching new behaviors through observational learning (modeling) has always been used in schools. Students have learned how to swing a bat, bend glass, cut a pattern, or pronounce a word in French through modeling. More recently, modeling has been used by teachers to demonstrate thinking skills, such as analyzing out loud the thought process involved in solving a math problem or demonstrating affective skills (such as dealing with students with learning or physical disabilities).

Bandura (1986) and Schunk (1987) have added new research to verify that modeling is an efficient way to acquire new behavior, especially when reinforcement and practice are key components. It has also been demonstrated that even peer models can be effective in teaching skills to classmates (Schunk & Hanson, 1985; Schunk, 2000).

IMPLEMENTATION

To teach through modeling, attention must be directed toward the desired behavior. These behaviors could involve procedures (lining up for lunch or dismissal), skills (threading a sewing machine), or mental processes (problem solving). It should be perfectly clear in the teacher's mind what steps are necessary to reach the desired behavior. The teacher should be able to explain and demonstrate the task. Throughout the demonstration, the students' attention should be focused on the task. The students should then be allowed to rehearse the task with constant feedback, both positive (reinforcing) and corrective (table 6.1).

MODELING

Table 6.1 Coaching Rubric for Modeling

Criteria (Descriptors)	Performance Indicators (Examples)
Preparation The teacher • identified the task to be achieved • analyzed the component parts of the task by breaking it into segments (steps) and sub-segments (sub-steps), when necessary • prepared a list of clear labels for the segments and sub-segments • prepared cards identifying each label	
Implementation • clarified the task for the students • checked to see if the students could restate the task (in their own words) • listed the steps necessary to completing the task • listed the sub-steps involved within each step, if the task called for it • demonstrated how to perform the task	
While performing, explained each step along the way • placed the corresponding label card next to each step • identified sub-steps • placed the corresponding label card next to each sub-step	
After performing, asked the students to identify the steps • identify the sub-steps • use the correct term (label) to identify each	
Student Practice The teacher • allowed each student to practice the task • provided positive feedback for each step implemented correctly • provided corrective feedback for steps implemented incorrectly	
During the practice, • asked the students to verbalize each step and sub-step • asked students to give positive and corrective feedback to each other • allowed enough practice time for mastery	

7

THE LECTURE

When you were a student, you experienced many lectures. What general impression do you have of lectures? Did you like learning this way? What made the difference between whether you learned anything in a lecture or not?

The lecture has been used for centuries. It transmits information by "covering" a lot of material, and the assumption is that what is said in the lecture is internalized by the listener. The lecture provides one-way communication in which students learn through one sense only—hearing. Listening to a lecture is an abstract way of learning and is, therefore, the least engaging.

MAKING LECTURES MORE ENGAGING

Research has demonstrated that the average student's attention span during a lecture is from 10 to 20 minutes, considerably less for younger students (Penner, 1984; Ryan et al., 2008), and that attention is cyclical (Ericksen, 1978). The student's attention (therefore, possibility for retention) is highest at the beginning of a 40- to 50-minute class, subsides considerably after the beginning, then increases to some degree just before the end.

This cycle is present even with a dynamic lecturer, though it was demonstrated that when actors delivered lectures as opposed to instructors, students achieved more (McLeskey & Waldron, 2004).

Think about the following:

> Lectures have bad reputations. Maybe you're familiar with the sayings, "telling is not teaching" and "the sage on the stage." Chinese proverbs tell us that "What I hear, I forget" and popular wall charts read "I remember 5% of what I hear, 10% of what I see." All of these sayings condemn us to using any modality other than telling. This is nonsense. It depends on *what* you tell and *how* you tell it." Hunter, 2004, p. 46. [italics in original]

The lecture integrates several different theories. You have already read some of them in earlier chapters. If a lecture is to be used, there are several ways to make it more effective for students (table 7.1).

- Know the material very well.
- Begin the lecture with a hook that involves the students. When you studied how to write a composition, you were told to make your first sentence an attention getter to capture the readers' interest. Do the same with listeners.
- Organize the material so that it can be presented in approximately 10-minute segments. This organization will make the next segment new again and take advantage of the 10-minute attention span of most students.
- Summarize important points at the end of each segment, or better, ask the students to summarize them. "The critical element of a lecture is to diagnose the amount of information students can process before they must interact with it" (Hunter, 2004, p. 47).
- Use visuals. They help clarify verbal content and assist students who are not auditory learners (Cruickshank et al., 2003).
- Provide vivid examples. When you read the concept attainment strategy in chapter 2, you noted how important clear examples were to learning concepts. Take advantage of using these clear examples to enhance students' understanding and involvement.
- Use advance organizers (chapter 4). These organizers put the content you present into perspective and assist the students in making associations with the content.

- Ask questions intermittently. Questions keep the students engaged and will give both you and them a means to determine how well content is being assimilated.
- Avoid reading your lecture. Prepare in advance key ideas you want to present, order of presentation, and important definitions and examples, then write them on index cards so that they are more readily visible. Before the lecture, rehearse what you want to say. Rehearsing your presentation out loud will help you clarify your own thinking. Avoiding reading your material verbatim will also allow you to use a more conversational tone in your delivery, keep eye contact with your students, and constantly monitor their reactions.
- Vary your presentation to avoid passive listening and attention loss (Wolvin, 1983). You can vary the stimuli by changing the pace, moving around the room, telling relevant but brief anecdotes, and using body language to convey important ideas and heighten emotional involvement.
- Remember that in a lecture, less is usually more. It is better that you cover less material that the students learn than a lot of material that does not get processed.
- Deliver your lecture with enthusiasm. It is contagious.

Table 7.1 Coaching Rubric for Lectures

Criteria (Descriptors)	Performance Indicators (Examples)
The teacher • prepared thoroughly the lecture content • introduced the lecture with a hook that engaged the students • organized the content in approximately 10-minute segments • organized the appropriate amount of material that could be processed • requested that the students summarize major points at the end of each segment • incorporated visuals • offered vivid examples • provided advance organizers • asked questions intermittently • varied presentation • delivered material without (major) reading time • presented material with enthusiasm	

Table 7.2 Teacher-Directed Strategies

Strategy	When To Use
Concept Attainment	To ensure that students can identify crucial attributes of a category (concept). This knowledge is a prerequisite for learning principles and solving problems
Concept Formation	To deepen understanding/discover new relationships at the end of a unit, chapter, story, novel
Advance Organizer	At beginning of a unit, novel, chapter, topic when a lot of verbal material is to be learned
Direct Instruction	When content or students need more structure and guidance
Modeling	To teach new skills (physical, thinking, or affective)
Lecture	To "cover" a lot of content

Table 7.2 is a summary of teacher-directed strategies and their use.

PART II SUMMARY

When using teacher-directed strategies, the teacher is generally in control of the content and methods of instruction. Teacher-directed strategies can be used with the whole class and with small groups.

When implementing concept attainment, the students identify attributes of concepts by comparing examples and contrasting them with non-examples.

During concept formation, students group attributes of concepts to identify what common attributes make up concepts.

The advanced organizer arranges concepts in a hierarchy with the most inclusive concept, the subsumer, at the top. The subsumer serves as a hook to which new learning is connected, thus giving it meaning.

Direct instruction is a highly structured model in which the teacher determines all content and methods of instruction delivered in small segments. The teacher keeps the students focused, paced, closely monitored, and actively engaged in academic learning to maximize allotted classroom time.

Modeling is a strategy used primarily for learning a new task, especially one requiring motor skills, by observing the performance of a model (the teacher). When using modeling, the teacher analyzes the task and breaks it into steps, explains and demonstrates the task, and allows the students to practice the task while they receive constant feedback.

The lecture is a one-way teaching strategy in which a lot of content is delivered. Students are involved as listeners and tend to tune out after a short time. To improve student engagement in lectures, they can be made more dynamic by incorporating visuals, advance organizers, vivid examples, asking intermittent questions, and summarizing content periodically.

III

STUDENT-CENTERED STRATEGIES

In the previous section, you reviewed strategies in which teachers exercise most of the control over the curriculum and its implementation. In this section, you will add to your repertoire the strategies that focus more on students' interests and give them more control over the content and choices of methodology. According to advocates of learner-centered strategies, this approach allows students to work at their own pace, develop self-direction, demonstrate their knowledge in different ways, and go beyond regular assignments offered in whole-class instruction.

8

PROBLEM-BASED LEARNING

THEORY

The seeds for problem-based learning were sown by some of the theorists with whom you are likely already familiar, as well as from education courses, such as Foundations of Education and Educational Psychology.

Dewey (1916), Thelen (1960), and Michaelis (1963) have given problem-based learning its philosophical thrust. They all believed in the idea that the school should be a miniature social system that reflects what citizens need to do to maintain a democratic society. In this mini social system, students face the same types of problems that citizens must solve, those that draw from all fields and utilize academic inquiry skills.

These methods are supported by cognitive and social psychologists. Piaget (1952) proposed that children must be actively involved in their own learning. Through this interaction, children construct representations regarding their experiences. With continued experiences, these representations in time become more sophisticated and abstract. Bruner (1961a) determined that the most important learning comes through personal discovery that occurs through active involvement in learning.

Vygotsky (1978) added the dimension of socio-cultural aspects in learning. He believed that to understand human activity, the context in which it occurs must be examined. Cognitive structures and thinking processes are created and developed in the social interaction within the culture. Social interactions with peers, as well as with adults, provide a means for "bouncing off" ideas that advance the student's cognitive development.

More recently, problem-based learning (PBL) received additional impetus from two more sources—medical education, to assist medical students in performing diagnoses (Barrows & Myers, 1997), and constructivism, with its emphasis on student-directed learning (Jones et al., 1997).

Teachers, often frustrated with the passive learning prevalent in schools, began looking for alternative ways of teaching other than by transmitting information through lectures, discussion, rote learning, and "covering" a wide curriculum by teaching subjects in isolation. They wanted an approach that would use higher thinking skills, through which students were involved in self-directed inquiry in decisions that affected their lives, and intrinsic motivation that would drive the learning process.

Brain research has verified that elaborative rehearsal (connecting new information to what we already know and reinforcing this information in several different ways) and "hands-on" activities are necessary for most learning and that studying a subject in isolation does not readily allow for the transfer of learning (Jensen, 1998).

An alternative method that fosters elaborative rehearsal, higher cognitive thinking, a deepening of understanding, and thematic instruction is problem-based learning. Several implementers of this strategy (Krajcik et al., 1999; Krajcik et al., 1994; Slavin et al., 1994; Blumenfeld et al., 1991) have placed their own imprints on the strategy while maintaining similar attributes. As you continue reading through problem-based learning, keep in mind how it reflects the philosophical, psychological, and social underpinnings mentioned previously, in addition to the medical (diagnostic) and constructivist (student-centered) applications.

IMPLEMENTATION

The underlying idea in problem-based learning is that the goal of education is not to have students do well in school, but to have them do well outside of school. Therefore, students are presented with a real problem, an authentic problem that is meaningful to them. The problem should be a challenging—one that adults wrestle with in the real world. If the problem is not authentic (does not actually affect the students personally and/or socially), it should at least be engaging.

The best problems are current. The problem could be offered by the teacher or suggested by the students. The problem might have a single solution or varied solutions, but the solution(s) must be genuine. The problem takes an extended time to complete, usually several weeks.

Once the problem is defined, it becomes the focus of instruction. Goals follow from the problem. Students learn different problem-solving skills. These could be the scientific method or a modified version, depending on the nature of the problem. The scientific method has several important steps.

- The problem is specified and students must understand all terms in the problem before they can go on.
- Tentative guesses (hypotheses) are offered to solve the problem.
- Each hypothesis is individually tested by gathering data.
- Each hypothesis is retested to check results.
- On the basis of hypothesis testing results, one or several hypotheses are selected to solve the problem.
- The solution is then implemented.
- The solution is monitored to see if it is producing the desired results.
- If not, this process is repeated until the problem is solved.

To test each hypothesis, data must be collected from several different subject areas, allowing students the opportunity to integrate knowledge from different disciplines. The students engage in a collaborative effort to collect and analyze data and select solutions. Collaboration itself is an important out-of-school mental activity with the problem providing a context for thinking (Resnick, 1987). Working together is also more motivational and develops social skills. Students may work in pairs or in another small group arrangement. As they work together, they share ideas, discuss solutions, and use real objects, such as computers, calculators, or scales.

The nature of the activities allows the students to construct their own meaning regarding real-world phenomena. The process in which they are engaged is as important as the solution.

When a solution is offered by a group, they must go beyond communicating this solution in the traditional forms, such as reports, dioramas, or collages. Students must produce authentic products to demonstrate what they have learned and how the problem was solved. Exhibits, videos, models, mock-ups, pamphlets, brochures, and computer programs are some examples of products the students can create. The products are then shared with the other groups who might have found different solutions.

The teacher's role is most crucial in determining the success of problem-based instruction. She serves as a coach and a model for the problem-solving skills her students will need (Stepien et al., 1997). She must ensure that students believe that they can solve the problem, have enough competence to do so, and can relate their success to effort. Attitudinal and verbal communication of the teacher is encouraging, and keeps the students' attention on the process involved in solving the problem, as well as in developing the end product.

Of equal importance is setting up a structure in the classroom that will ensure success. This structure necessitates that the teacher provides access to materials to assist the students in the investigating, monitors the interaction between or among students, and encourages students to think for themselves and express their points of view.

The teacher must be able to manage logistical and organizational problems to ensure that work flows smoothly. Where will materials be stored? How can the environment where many different groups are working on different tasks be controlled? What types of arrangements must be made for out-of-class research the students must conduct in the school library (or with resource people or places within the community itself)? If one or several groups finish early, how can they be kept involved until the other groups complete their work?

IN SUMMARY

PBL is an instructional method that uses a real-world problem as the context for an in-depth investigation of core content. The problems that students tackle are ill-structured; they include just enough information to suggest how students should proceed with an investigation, but never enough information to enable students to solve the problem without further inquiry. These problems cannot be solved by using formulas—students must use the inquiry process and reasoning—and there may be more than one way to solve the problem. Teachers who use a problem-based learning approach become tutors or coaches, helping students understand their own thinking and guiding them as they search for new information. Through problem-based learning, students become better problem solvers because they hone skills such as reasoning, collaboration, and persistence in their self-directed search for solutions (Stepien, 1997, p. 111).

Though there are many positive characteristics of problem-based learning, there are also several concerns. Given the organizational school structures and prevalent time for meeting state learning standards, problem-based learning is a difficult strategy to implement.

The strategy needs the support of library and technological resources, which can be expensive. Only a limited amount of information can be covered using this approach. Grading of students' work is a persistent issue. And finally, the teacher must have the knowledge to be able to draw from many different disciplines and the managerial skills to keep the students on target (table 8.1).

Table 8.1 Coaching Rubric for Problem-Based Learning (T)

Criteria (Descriptors)	Performance Indicators (Examples)

The teacher
- presented students with a developmentally appropriate problem
- presented students with an authentic problem
- presented a problem solvable in more than one way
- presented a problem capable of being solved through drawing on several disciplines
- explained the scientific method for problem solving
- provided practice in the scientific method for problem solving
- assisted each student in determining what contribution he or she would make in helping solve the problem
- provided adequate resources and materials for solving the problem
- explained how the resources and materials could be used
- established a system for storing materials
- assisted students in selecting partners or small groups
- encouraged students to discuss and explore
- encouraged students to express their ideas
- kept students focused on work
- assisted students in determining suitable final products
- allowed students to share and present their final products

SERVICE LEARNING

Service learning is a type of problem-based learning that began to gain popularity more than two decades ago as community service. Though it started in colleges and universities, service learning is now being used increasingly in high schools, and even in middle and elementary schools.

Service learning is not a strategy with the characteristics of those you have previously studied; it is a learner-centered problem-based technique that involves Dewey's concepts of "learning by doing" and the responsibilities of citizenship. It is different from an internship or general field experience in that service learning is a project where public service is the focus. The service must be provided for a nonprofit organization or a profit organization offering service on a pro bono basis. For example, a lawyer might take a case for a client who could not afford payment and the lawyer would waive the service fee.

Service learning is individualized because the student selects the type of public service and project with which she would like to be involved. It is interactive because the student implements the learning in the field as opposed to in the classroom. The field could be at a special program or service agency. Service learning offers a dual benefit for both the participants who volunteer and the clients of the agency as they focus on what they have to offer each other (Kendall & Associates, 1990).

Service learning has become more structured regarding its outcomes. For the link between academic study and the service component to be effective,

- the problem(s) the volunteer (student) deals with must be real.
- the main goals and objectives of the service project must be clear so that the student involved knows what specific project and sets of activities must be undertaken.
- the goals and objectives of the service project must be age appropriate.
- initial contact between the service agency personnel and the school instructor must be established to ensure that the needs of all are being met, that the objectives and activities of the service project can be achieved in that environment, and to identify any legal issues for all parties.
- a contract should be signed by the agency and the school instructor.

- the school instructor should maintain regular contact with the service agency to monitor student progress and ensure that the contract terms are implemented.
- the student should keep an anecdotal record of activities, problems, and questions.
- a decision should be made in advance regarding how the service learning project will be evaluated.

Service learning may be implemented in the community at large as long as the project addresses genuine community needs (Fertman et al., 1996). Whatever the setting, service learning assists the student in integrating theory and practice in a content area to deepen her understanding of the subject. Most important, she must apply her knowledge to work effectively and solve problems. Students are encouraged to develop independent thinking and research skills. For example, a student who is working in a soup kitchen might study the sociological, cultural, and historical/political policies that contribute to or alleviate hunger.

Many teachers and students still feel ill at ease in dealing with the many difficulties involved with societal problems. Parents are frequently wary about having their children interacting with some of the agencies that would support the academic component. The decision to embark on a service learning project is difficult, but the rewards are often well worth the effort (Kottler & Kottler, 2000). Table 8.2 offers the service learning coaching rubric.

Table 8.2 Coaching Rubric for Service Learning (T)

Criteria (Descriptors)	Performance Indicators (Examples)
The teacher	
• identified with student a real (authentic) problem	
• clarified with student objectives and activities needed to solve problem	
• arranged with student in advance that an anecdotal record of activities, problems, and questions was to be kept	
• decided with student before beginning the project how it would be evaluated	
• established initial contact with all involved parties (social agency personnel and school instructor) to ensure that project objectives and activities could be achieved within the assigned environment	
• identified legal issues for all involved	
• arranged that a contract between the agency and school liaison be signed before beginning	
• scheduled regular contact between social agency and school to monitor student progress according to contract	

9

COOPERATIVE LEARNING

Cooperative learning is often used synonymously with group instruction. However, cooperative learning is not just any type of grouping, but a specific method of group instruction. If an advance organizer (chapter 4) were to be formed to explain different types of groupings, group instruction would be the subsumer (the more inclusive term) and cooperative learning would be classified under group instruction.

Cooperative learning is essentially "students working together in a group small enough so that everyone can participate on a collective task that has been clearly defined, and without direct and immediate supervision by the teacher" (Cohen, 1994, p. 3). In cooperative learning, groups compete with each other and individuals within groups compete with their past performance.

THEORY

As you read in the previous section on problem-based learning, John Dewey (1916) envisioned the classroom as a miniature democratic society where positive social and interpersonal relationships among citizens would be necessary for the success of the society. His philosophical vision occurred at a time when whites dominated the society.

As racial integration gained acceptance, it became clear that more had to be done than passing laws to make integration work. Prejudice had to be counteracted in some way, not only among ethnic groups but also against people with disabilities and new immigrants. Sharan (1992) put forth the idea that prejudice could be reduced if different ethnic groups were allowed direct contact without intermediaries, and if this contact occurred in an officially approved environment that offered equal status.

The major researchers who capitalized on the ideas of Dewey (1916) and Sharan (1992) and who contributed to the development of an educational environment that would improve social interaction and interpersonal relationships are Slavin (1987) and Johnson & Johnson (1991). The strategy is known as *cooperative learning*. It commonly follows a teacher-directed lesson and is geared for both academic and social success.

Cooperative learning has several essential attributes that ensure against the traditional criticisms of groups in which a few students participate and other slough off, taking little if any responsibility, where some students dominate and there could be in-fighting. The essential attributes of cooperative learning are: positive interdependence, face-to-face interaction, individual accountability, collaborative skills, and group processing (Johnson & Johnson, 1999).

1. *Positive interdependence.* Learners in the group have a dual role. They are responsible for their own achievement, as well as for the achievement of every other member of the group. Each member depends on every other member for success.
2. *Face-to-face interaction.* Each learner contributes to the learning of every other member through coaching, encouraging, evaluating, and motivating. The incentive for doing so is winning team honors for reaching new levels of individual growth. Team honors are based on growth determined by improvement of prior performance.
3. *Individual accountability.* Though team members practice together and coach each other, everyone is individually tested. The group can succeed only when every member has learned the objective. Because the individual learning gains of each member (individual improvement over prior performance) form the basis

of the team score, it is in the vested interest of everyone in the group for each member to achieve.
4. *Collaborative skills.* For the group to succeed, they must learn mutual assistance skills, such as dealing with disputes, communicating, problem solving, acceptance, and trust.
5. *Group processing.* The group takes the initiative in reflecting on their achievement and interaction to improve performance the next time around.

For the group to succeed academically and socially, the team members must be arranged heterogeneously. Depending on the make-up of a class, a group of five or six would be mixed by gender and achievement as well as by social class, culture, and ethnicity. A non-English–speaking student could even be a part of the team.

Team rewards offer an incentive for higher-achieving students to coach lower-ability students. In doing so, the higher-achieving students identify their own need for understanding as they attempt to clarify their thinking when explaining material to others. Coaching reinforces the content for the high achiever and assists him in attaining mastery. (However, some research [Fuchs et al. (1998), and Robinson & Clinkenbeard, (1998)] has concluded that gifted students tend to achieve more when they are placed in groups with other gifted or high-ability students.)

Lower-ability students are motivated to work harder and achieve for the benefit of the group. This achievement not only breaks the cycle of failure but also serves as a motivator to continue to achieve.

New social bonds are created as students offer each other mutual assistance. Students who might have been viewed as "nerds" now become valuable resources. Popular students who did not achieve academically are no longer viewed as assets in contributing to the group and are forced to face their academic voids. Less-accepted students separated by social class find themselves interacting positively with other group members in non-classroom settings.

IMPLEMENTATION

Before the cooperative learning group goes into action, the teacher presents a lesson or series of lessons, usually to the whole class. From that content, she develops a packet for the cooperative learning group. The packet usually contains:

- objectives that clearly state what each member of the group is to accomplish
- exercises (instructional activities) to develop the objectives
- materials for completing the instructional activities
- a preliminary assessment of the objectives
- rules for behavior within the group (which may be developed with the students before the group work begins).

Leighton (2006) suggested some guidelines:

1. Work quietly together on team assignments.
2. Ask for and give explanations, not answers.
3. Listen carefully to teammates' questions.
4. Ask teammates for help if you need it.
5. Work at the pace that is right for your team.
6. Help each other stay on task; don't talk about or work on other things.
7. Remember that the team's work is finished only when every member knows the material.
8. Ask the teacher for help only after you have asked everyone on your own team (p. 314).

The structure provided by the teacher in the packet is a crucial determinant of the successful achievement of the objectives. Group members then begin to work together by coaching each other and checking each other's work until all achieve the objectives. Finally, a test is administered to each group member individually, and the team score is based on individual improvement over prior performance.

After a considerable amount of achievement and bonding have resulted within the group, groups can be changed to forge new relationships.

Johnson & Johnson (1994) reported that cooperative learning produced greater academic achievement than that in competitive or individualized strategies, improved social interaction among students, and higher positive attitudes toward academic subjects and school in general. To implement cooperative learning, use the coaching rubric, table 9.1.

Table 9.1 Coaching Rubric for Cooperative Learning (T)

Criteria (Descriptors)	Performance Indicators (Examples)
The teacher • presented first the content (lesson or lessons) to entire class • designed a clear procedure (packet) for completing a task relevant to the content • provided to all students group guidelines that were discussed and rehearsed • structured groups for heterogeneity (gender, achievement, student disabilities, cultural, ethnic, and language diversity) • prepared an individual assessment for mastery of content without assistance from peers in group • presented a reward to each group that achieved a predetermined standard of individual gain averages	

JIGSAW

Jigsaw is a variation of the previous cooperative learning strategy. As in the prior strategy, the students are divided into diverse groups of 5 or 6. However, the content to be learned in the jigsaw model is separated into small chunks, each of which is a piece of the content jigsaw puzzle. If the Civil War was to be covered, for example, these chunks could be society of the North; society of the South; battle plan of the North; battle plan of the South; Civil War timeline; war aftereffects, or any other way the teacher might choose to organize the content.

Each student in the group is assigned one of these chunks and becomes an "expert" on the topic. They then meet with students from different groups who have been assigned the same topic. These students discuss and refine their knowledge and organize a coherent comprehensive presentation, which they rehearse. This group does not disband until all are clear and satisfied with the content and how they will deliver it. The students then rejoin their original groups and teach that content to the other members.

Eventually, each student teaches his or her content. This communication is the only way the other group members will be able to access the material. They must, therefore, pay attention and ensure that they absorb the information from the "expert" because at the end of the presentations, all will be tested to achieve a group score.

To facilitate the work of the group, one student is assigned to be the leader. The leader role is rotated when different topics are studied. The teacher's role is to monitor the groups by circulating among them to ensure that all understand their responsibilities and are working effectively.

Jigsaw offers a challenging way to learn content. It provides a way for each student to play an essential part in the learning process while fostering group member dependency through listening and interaction to achieve a high group score. The Coaching Rubric for Jigsaw is presented in table 9.2.

Table 9.2 Coaching Rubric for Jigsaw (T)

Criteria (Descriptors)	Performance Indicators (Examples)
The teacher • divided students into diverse groups of five or six members • prepared a topic in small segments equal to the number of students in the group • assigned a leader from each group to facilitate group work on the topic • appointed one student in each group to master one segment of the topic • allowed student time to master the content individually • formed a group of experts from students assigned the same segment • allowed time for the experts to study, refine, and rehearse their content presentation • asked the students to join their original groups • invited each student to teach his or her segment to the original group • encouraged other group members to question the expert to make sure they understood the content • circulated among groups to assess problems • presented a test on the topic	

10

MASTERY LEARNING

THEORY

Mastery learning is a type of individualized instruction which assumes that almost all students are capable of mastery (high achievement) given sufficient time and the correct instruction. Its roots are in behavior theory with its focus on specific learning objectives, small units of instruction presented at a time, and immediate feedback and rewards for accomplishment.

It appears as though personalized (mastery) learning, predominant in the '60s and '70s, is being rediscovered.

> The elements of 21st-century learning are part of personalized learning, but added to these is the more revolutionary component of a competency-based, time variable model in which students progress at their own pace as skills are mastered, rather than advancing through grade levels with peers. The rise of personalized learning in districts across the nation can be attributed to a convergence of multiple circumstances, including technological advances, nearly ubiquitous digital content, the Obama administration's support for school innovation, and the growing willingness of states to grant waivers for mandated "seat time" requirements and, in (some) cases . . . to eliminate those requirements altogether (McLester, 2011).

Benjamin Bloom (1968, 1976) is the major proponent of mastery learning. Bloom's work, based on prior work by Carroll (1963), has demonstrated that mastery learning permits approximately 80 percent of students to attain a level of achievement ordinarily reached by only 20 percent using other methods. The challenge persists regarding what to do with the remaining students who do not achieve mastery.

Mastery learning employs certain *assumptions* and implies a specific instructional model. It assumes that

- quality learning is possible for most, if not all students
- for quality learning to take place, the instruction must change
- some students may need more time than others
- most learning follows sequential and logical steps
- most learning outcomes can be expressed in observable and measurable terms
- students can be successful at each level of instruction, thus providing them with the incentive to advance further

IMPLEMENTATION

In the model, the instruction is individualized. The teacher ensures that certain features are present in the instructional design. The student's knowledge is pre-assessed to pinpoint areas of weakness.

This pre-assessment is often referred to as a diagnostic test or pre-test. The teacher discusses the results of the pre-test with the student and together they decide what goals and objectives would be desirable to improve performance. The objectives are stated in specific, behavioral terms.

A signed contract is set up between student and teacher agreeing how the objectives will be implemented, how often the teacher will check work, and how long it should take the student to complete the contract. Older students will be able to spend more sequential time working on the contract than younger students. Input regarding how the student likes to learn is also received at this point, and the teacher makes every effort to include the student's suggestions as part of the instructional component.

A personalized packet is designed for the student. This packet, also referred to as a learning activity package (LAP) or a self-instructional package (SIP), contains the objectives or small set of objectives, specific practice activities the student performs to achieve the objectives, and an assessment to inform the student how well she is meeting the objectives. The activities are structured and expressed clearly enough so that the student can implement them without the teacher's presence, leaving the teacher free to work with other groups or individual students.

To ensure that the contract is personalized, directions and instruction should be written in a conversational tone. "You will be able to add fractions with unlike denominators" is more personal than "The student will be able to . . . " For students who cannot read yet, the instructions can be prepared on tape.

The instructional activities should be engaging, varied, attractive, and include auditory, visual, and tactile/kinesthetic modalities. These could include computers, manipulatives, videos, magazines/newspapers, models, and diagrams. If, after working on the practice activities, the objectives have still not been met, corrective instruction is provided (instruction is recycled) until the objectives have been attained. It should be obvious that if a student does not achieve the objective using one instructional activity, a different instructional activity must be made available.

The student is then allowed to continue to work on the remaining sets of objectives with immediate feedback and recycling, if necessary. After the student has completed all of the objectives, she takes a post-test to determine how well she has mastered the material.

In many cases, the pre-test and post-test are the same, and there should be an appreciable difference in achievement demonstrated in the post-test. If not, a new contract is established with different instructional strategies.

Self-instructional packages do not necessarily have to be designed for remediation. They can also be used as enrichment for students who need challenge, or as make-up work for students who missed class due to absence or visits to the psychologist, speech therapist, instrumental music teacher, or any other member of the school staff.

Mastery learning is particularly effective when the student needs to develop concepts or skills that serve as a foundation for additional learning. See the Coaching Rubric for Mastery Learning, table 10.1, to help you implement this strategy.

Table 10.1 Coaching Rubric for Mastery Learning (T)

Criteria (Descriptors)	Performance Indicators (Examples)
The teacher • administered a diagnostic test (pre-test)* • established goals and objectives of instruction (preferably with the student, when age appropriate) on the basis of test results • prepared a packet with a set of sequenced objectives grouped in small segments • secured ideas for activities from the student's suggestions • prepared varieties of activities to meet the objectives (integrated different learning modalities) • prepared packet using unique formats and designs to make it more attractive to the student • wrote directions and instructional activities using the pronoun "you" • prepared an assessment for each objective (though one assessment could cover several objectives) • determined with the student a realistic daily schedule and time frame for completion If a contract evolved, • signed the contract and had student sign the contract • determined a reward for successful completion of the contract • administered a post-test to determine achievement If the post-test did not demonstrate growth • prepared an alternative activity for each unachieved objective • filed packet for future use for a student with similar needs (no need to reinvent the wheel)	

* When using the packet for enrichment or for make-up work, the diagnostic test would not need to be administered.

Computer-Assisted Instruction (CAI)

Closely related to the behavioral themes that form the foundation for mastery learning is a unique form of interactive individualized instruction, computer-assisted instruction (CAI). Therefore, it would be remiss not to at least mention the effect of computers on individualized instruction. With this kind of instruction, students, using computer programs (programmed instruction), can work at their own level and at their own pace.

In the '60s and '70s, CAI provided a student with a teaching machine that included earphones and a TV screen. The student would type in his name or identification number and the machine would welcome him by saying, "Hi, Paul, welcome to learning about multiplication facts. If that is O.K. with you, type 'Yes' then press Enter. If not, press 'No' then press Enter." If the student agreed, the machine would ask a question (the stimulus) and the student would type an answer (the response). The student would then receive immediately either reinforcing or corrective feedback. The program used could keep track of Paul's work for the teacher in the form of a printout, and move to additional instruction by changing the sequence and difficulty of the activities before proceeding to the next lesson.

In this form, most of CAI was useful for drill-and-practice objectives.

But with the advent of the relatively inexpensive microcomputer, CAI was able to be used by more students for additional purposes. Many schools now have computer labs with multiple computers in each lab, and most classrooms have at least one computer.

With further development, CAI expanded its use from presenting questions or problems, receiving responses, and providing feedback to offering tutorials, simulations, and educational games. *Simulations* go beyond drill and practice by engaging students in real-life and problem-solving activities. Students must formulate tentative solutions, test each solution, and, if not successful, come up with more solutions. *Games* allow students to reinforce learning or develop higher levels of learning. Many students also select games as a reward for either exhibiting proper behavior or achieving a certain level of subject mastery.

As you already know, the Internet is revolutionizing classroom instruction. More and more school districts are connecting to the Internet, permitting their computers to communicate with other computers throughout the world. Students can communicate within the school, as well as with schools in other states and countries via e-mail, social networks, and videoconferencing applications. Students can take courses and even entire degrees through distance learning.

The World Wide Web provides a universe of information available through many large computer networks joined together, from which information can be accessed instantly not only in school but at home. As a result, students can collaborate on research projects and problem solving. Students can also work at their own pace on completing assignments and do research on topics of individual interest.

In order to do research, students can also access sources of information, not specific information, from directories or search engines. These directories search appropriate websites to match a request for information with that available from the directory.

Some directories (search engines) relevant to the different age and cognitive levels of your students are: (http://www.bing.com); (http://www.ask.com); (http://www.google.com); (http://www.yahoo.com); and (http://www.dogpile.com).

Many teachers are now using handheld computers to enrich content by connecting with other teachers and sources. These computers assist teachers in providing their students with learning activities in all curriculum areas using technology that supports data analysis, thinking, and data retrieval (Staudt, 2005).

Students are also using digital devices to record their own stories, along with videos they have made that can be shared on a school's website as well as on the Internet. Students can then watch their videos to self-correct content as well as speech, grammar, and delivery.

Personal digital assistants (PDAs) can help students (and teachers) track tasks, assignments, and other important information. Smart phones combine color screens with a mobile phone and Internet access into one lightweight and small hand-held device. Smart phones offer a multi-touch screen with full-screen web browsing, e-mail access, and video playback.

Computer technology is a valuable resource for research, reinforcement, and enrichment and should be infused into the curriculum. But as with all resources, it should complement and supplement the teacher's role and help tailor information for each learner's needs. With its access to text, sound, graphics, simulation, and animation, computer technology has the potential to lead students to higher learning levels and engage them in brain-compatible active learning using multiple pathways.

Computer technology is expanding exponentially and becoming increasingly interactive. It is not unusual for students to have greater knowledge of computers and their applications than teachers. Many students possess a cognitive level of sophistication that enables them to design their own computer programs. Computer literacy is crucial for both students and teachers. Teachers must keep up with this explosive technology, which, like it or not, is slowly changing the way they teach.

LEARNING ACTIVITY CENTERS (LEARNING STATIONS)

Learning activity centers (LACs) are miniature versions of the open classroom. In the open classroom, the curriculum is not set or delivered by the teacher in a formal sense, but rather by developmentally appropriate materials placed in the classroom.

Students decide the materials with which they would like to engage. The role of the teacher is to track what the student is doing and intercede to ensure that learning is occurring as a result of the engagement. On the basis of what the students are achieving, the materials are changed so that students can continue interacting with new materials and grow and learn from that process.

THEORY

The open classroom received its main impetus from the Progressive Movement spurred by the work of John Dewey (1916) and was further promoted as an instructional method by educators because of the developmental theory of Piaget (1954). Dewey saw education as a process that provided experience and action rather than a focus on purely academic work. He saw education as holistic, where the whole student, including particular interests and abilities, had to be taken into account before planning any curriculum and instruction.

An environment had to be set up in which students had to actively participate in their own learning. The curriculum had to be child-centered, where the child learned by doing.

Piaget believed that humans inherit the ability for organization and adaptation. During the organization process, students make sense of their world by gathering and arranging their information into psychological structures. With continued experience these structures are further combined and coordinated to form more sophisticated structures (schemas) which help us "think about" the objects and events that occur in the environment.

Humans also have the inherent ability to adapt to their environment. They do this through *assimilation* and *accommodation*. In assimilation, humans use their existing psychological structures when they come in contact with new information or experience that fits with what they already know. In accommodation, humans must adjust their existing psychological structures to respond to new information or a new situation. Assimilation and accommodation are constantly used as people face increasingly complex environments.

The open classroom responds to the interactive, experiential environments supported by Dewey and Piaget. However, when open classrooms were implemented in the '20s and '30s and rediscovered in the '70s, they were not successful in providing needed knowledge and skills. Many schools that were built with open designs gradually had those designs replaced by walls that separated classes in the same way as they were in more traditional education.

IMPLEMENTATION

The LAC provides a modification that can be used to reap the positive effects of the open classroom while maintaining for the rest of the class more structured approaches. Also known as a learning station, the learning activity center is a sectioned-off location within the classroom. There may be more than one station in the room. Students usually work at the center individually, though they may work in pairs or other small groups.

LEARNING ACTIVITY CENTERS (LEARNING STATIONS) 73

The center can be used for enrichment, reinforcing information after a lesson, making up work, interacting with new content when a task is completed, or for remediation. The teacher provides all materials students need in order to work at the center. Since the center is self-contained in this respect, the student can work alone without the teacher's presence, though the center is often supervised by a para-professional.

Unless the center is designed for an exploratory activity where the students can work with materials to see if there is anything unique they can come up with, *the center needs structure*. This structure is often presented in the form of a chart, poster, activity cards, or audio/videotape which gives instructions regarding how the materials are to be used.

Dewey (1938) warned educators that there was a *difference between an activity and an experience*. His warning was again addressed by Hutchings & Wurtzdorff (1988).

Dewey noted that students can be working with materials, being involved with an *activity* indefinitely. But it is the teacher's role to make sure the activity is turned into an *experience*, which Dewey defined as making a connection with the activity and the learning that the activity should produce.

For example, a student can be playing with tongue depressors (pipe cleaners, toothpicks) placing them one on top of the other and making different types of designs for a long time, and that has some value. But the teacher should ensure that the student can count ten tongue depressors, put a rubber band around them, leaving him or her with one group of tens. He or she can then slide the tongue depressors out of the rubber band to get back his or her ten groups of one.

If the teacher did not provide this structure, the student might play with the tongue depressors without ever realizing that one group of ten is the same as ten ones. This regrouping is an essential prerequisite to addition and subtraction of two-digit numerals.

Thus the activity, playing with the tongue depressors, was turned into an experience, learning that one group of ten (one ten) and ten groups of one (ten ones) are two different names for the same number, ten. Therefore, the instructions provided by the teacher in the center ensure that the learning objective(s) the teacher has in mind for having the students engaged with the materials at the center are achieved.

To set up a learning activity center, use the Coaching Rubric for Orga-

Table 11.1 Coaching Rubric for Organizing Learning Activity Centers

Criteria (Descriptors)	Performance Indicators (Examples)
The teacher • decided the purpose for setting up the LAC (specific cognitive knowledge, discovery, exploration, enrichment, review, skill development, etc.) • related the topic of the LAC to the current curriculum • determined the specific objectives of the LAC • informed the students of the purpose of the LAC • prepared an attractive LAC • selected materials that integrated several disciplines, whenever possible • provided a variety of materials appropriate for achieving the objectives • provided safe materials • posted clear instructions and activities for using materials • arranged for the LAC to be supervised by an aide/volunteer	

Table 11.2 Student-Centered Strategies

Strategy	When to Use
Problem-Based Learning	Solve appropriate authentic problems suited to the developmental level of students
Service Learning	Solve a problem that addresses a genuine community need
Cooperative Learning	Increase achievement by having small groups compete with each other and individuals within groups compete with their past performance
Mastery Learning	Provide tailor-made individualized instruction that is self-correcting
Learning Activity Center	Offer individual students new material, enrichment, reinforcement, makeup work, remediation, or a free time assignment

nized Learning Activity Centers, table 11.1. Table 11.2 is a summary of student-centered strategies and their use.

PART III SUMMARY

Problem-based learning is a group method for solving real (authentic) problems. The group draws from several subjects, uses inquiry and reasoning to solve problems that could have several solutions, and designs a final product that demonstrates what they have learned. The teacher serves as a guide who structures resources to help students in their explorations and helps students understand their own thinking.

LEARNING ACTIVITY CENTERS (LEARNING STATIONS)

When implementing service learning, a student conducts a structured public service project for the purpose of solving a real problem. Clear project goals, objectives, and activities are established in advance, as well as the method of evaluating the project. In order to solve the problem, the student integrates theory and practice in a subject area, thus developing deeper understanding, independent thinking, and research skills.

Cooperative learning is a specific type of group instruction which follows whole class instruction. The group is set up heterogeneously for both social and academic growth. Students demonstrate responsibility for their own growth as well as for the growth of every other group member by coaching, motivating, and evaluating each other. Individual improvement over prior performance determines the group score. The group with the greatest achievement receives a reward. The teacher provides the group with structure by designing a packet containing objectives, materials, and an assessment.

Jigsaw is a type of cooperative learning strategy in which one student in each group becomes an expert on one segment of a topic. Students from different groups with the same segment discuss and share information on this segment and prepare a presentation. These group members then join their original groups to teach the information to other group members, who are eventually tested to attain a group score.

Mastery learning delivers individualized instruction in small, sequential segments with immediate feedback and alternative corrective feedback, when necessary, until objectives are achieved. Growth is determined by the difference in performance between pre- and post-test performance and is followed by a reward for appreciable results. The teacher designs a learning activity package with enough structure so that the student can work independently.

Computer-assisted instruction offers tutorials, simulations, and educational games to enhance instruction. With computers students can do research on the Internet and use e-mail and chat rooms to communicate with other students around the world. Courses and entire degrees are offered through distance learning.

The learning activity center can be used for enrichment, reinforcement, make-up work, remediation, or for learning new content. At the center, students can work alone or in small groups by interacting with materials. The teacher provides a structure such as a chart, poster, activity cards, or audiotape which instructs the students how to use the materials to ensure that learning results.

REFERENCES

INTRODUCTION

Joyce, B, & Showers, B. (2002). *Student achievement through staff development,* 3rd ed., Alexandria, VA: Association for Supervision and Curriculum Development.

Marzano, R. J. (2002). *Research-based strategies for increasing student achievement.* Audiotape #203062. Alexandria: VA, Association for Supervision and Curriculum Development.

PART I

Brookhart, S. M. (2004). *Grading.* Upper Saddle River, NJ: Pearson Education.

Danielson, C. (2007). *Enhancing professional practice: A framework for teaching,* 2nd ed. Alexandria, VA: Association for Supervision and Curriculum Development.

Danielson, C., & McGreal, T. (2000). *Teacher evaluation to enhance professional practice.* Alexandria, VA: Association for Supervision and Curriculum Development.

Danielson, C. (1996). *Enhancing professional practice: A framework for teaching.* Alexandria, VA: Association for Supervision and Curriculum Development.

Delpit, L. (1995). *Other people's children: Cultural conflict in the classroom.* New York: The New Press.

Good, T., & Brophy, J. (1974). Changing teacher and student behavior: An empirical investigation. *Journal of Educational Psychology*, 66, 390–405.

Hook, C., & Rosenshine, B. (1979). Accuracy of teacher reports of their classroom behavior. *Review of Educational Research*, 49, 1–12.

Joyce, B., & Showers, B. (1995). *Student achievement through staff development*, 2nd ed. New York: Longman.

Joyce, B., & Showers, B. (2002). *Student achievement through staff development*, 3rd ed., Alexandria, VA: Association for Supervision and Curriculum Development.

Lazear, D. (1998). *The rubrics way: Using MI to assess understanding.* Tuscon, AZ: Zephyr Press.

Reiman, A., & Thies-Sprinthall, L. (1998). *Mentoring and supervision for teacher development.* New York: Longman.

Sadker, M., & Sadker, D. (1994). *Failing at fairness: How America's schools cheat girls.* New York: Scribner.

Welch, J. (2000). *GE strategy and performance . . . as reported to share owners 1980 to 2000.* Fairfield, CT: GE Corporation.

Wiggins, G. (1998). *Sophisticated & naïve vs. right & wrong: How to assess for intellectual progress.* Audiotape #298303. Alexandria, VA: Association for Supervision and Curriculum Development.

Wiggins, G. (2005). *Educative assessment*, 2nd ed. Alexandria, VA: Association for Supervision and Curriculum Development.

Wolfe, P. (2001). *Brain matters: Translating research into classroom practice.* Alexandria, VA: Association for Supervision and Curriculum Development.

PART II

Anderson, J. R., Reder, L. M., & Simon, H. A. (1996). Situated learning and education. *Educational Researcher*, 25, 5–11.

Ausubel, D. P. (1963). *The psychology of meaningful verbal learning.* New York: Grune and Stratton.

Ausubel, D. P. (1977). The facilitation of meaningful verbal learning in the classroom. *Educational Psychologist.* 12, 162–78.

Ausubel, D. P., Novak, J. D., & Hanesian, H. (1978). *Educational psychology: A cognitive view.* New York: Holt, Rinehart, & Winston.

Bandura, A. (1969). *Principles of behavior modification.* New York: Holt, Rinehart, & Winston.

REFERENCES

Bandura, A. (ed.) (1974). *Psychological modeling: Conflicting theories.* New York: Lieber-Atherton.

Bandura, A. (1986). *Social foundations of thought and action.* Englewood Cliffs, NJ: Prentice-Hall.

Bandura, A., & Walters, R. H. (1963). *Social learning and personality development.* New York: Holt, Rinehart, & Winston.

Benjafield, J. G. (1992). *Cognition.* Englewood Cliffs, NJ: Prentice Hall.

Berg, C. A., & Clough, M. (1991). Hunter lesson design: the wrong one for science teaching. *Educational Leadership*, 48 (4), pp. 73–78.

Bruner, J. S., Goodnow, J. J., & Austin, G. A. (1967). *A study of thinking.* New York: Wiley.

Chall, J. (1999). *The academic achievement challenge: What really works in the classroom.* New York: Guilford Press.

Covington, M. V., & Beery, R. G. (1976). *Self-worth and school learning.* New York: Holt, Rinehart, & Winston.

Cruickshank, D., Bainer Jenkins, D., & Metcalf, K. (2003). *The act of teaching,* 3rd ed. Boston: McGraw-Hill

Davis, G. A. (1983). *Educational psychology: Theory and practice.* Reading, MA: Addison-Wesley.

Ellis, A. (2001). *Research on educational innovations,* 3rd ed. Larchmont, NY: Eye on Education.

Ericksen, S .C. (1978). *The lecture: Memo to the faculty,* no. 60. Ann Arbor: Center for Research on Teaching and Learning, University of Michigan.

Fisher, C. W., Filby, N. N., & Marliave, R. (1977). *Descriptions and distributions of ALT within and across classes during the B-C period.* Technical note IV-b. San Francisco: Far West Laboratory for Educational Research and Development.

Gagne, E. D., Yekovick, C. W., & Yekovick, F. R. (1993). *The cognitive psychology of school learning,* 2nd ed. New York: HarperCollins.

Hunter, R. (2004). *Madeline Hunter's mastery teaching: Increasing instructional effectiveness in elementary and secondary schools.* Updated ed. Thousand Oaks, CA: Corwin Press.

Joyce B., & Weil, M. (2000). *Models of teaching,* 6th ed. Needham Heights, MA: Allyn & Bacon.

Joyce, B., Weil, M., with Calhoun, E. (2004). *Models of teaching,* 7th ed. Boston: Pearson.

Marzano, R. J. (2002). *Research-based strategies for increasing student achievement.* Audiotape #203062. Alexandria: VA: Association for Supervision and Curriculum Development.

McDonald, F. J. (1976). Report on phase II of the beginning teacher evaluation study. *Journal of Teacher Education,* 27, 39–42.

McLeskey, J., & Waldron, N. (2004). Three conceptions of teacher learning: Exploring the relationship between knowledge and the practice of teaching. *Teacher Education and Special Education*, 27(1), 3–14.

Miller, N. E. & Dollard, J. (1941). *Social learning and imitation*. New Haven: Yale University Press.

Penner, J. G. (1984). *Why many college teachers cannot lecture*. Springfield, IL: Thomas.

Rosch, E. H. (1973). On the internal structure of perceptual and semantic categories. In T. Moore (ed.), *Cognitive development and the acquisition of language*, pp. 111–44. New York: Academic Press

Rosenshine B., & Furst, N. E. (1971). Research on teacher performance criteria. In B. O. Smith (ed.). *Research in teacher education: A symposium*. Englewood Cliffs, NJ: Prentice-Hall.

Rosenshine B., & Furst, N. E. (1973). The use of direct observation to study teaching. In R. Travers (ed.), *Second handbook of research on teaching*. Chicago: Rand McNally.

Rosenshine B. (1979). Content, time, and direct instruction. In P. Peterson & H. Walberg (eds.), *Research on teaching: Concepts, findings, and implications*, pp. 28–56. Berkeley, CA: McCutchan.

Rosenshine B. (1985). Direct instruction. In T. Husen, and T. N. Postelwath (eds.), *International encyclopedia of education*, 3, 1395–1400. Oxford: Pergamon Press.

Rosenshine B. (1995). Advances in research on instruction. *Journal of Educational Research*, 88(5), 262–68.

Ryan, K., Cooper, J., & Tauer, S. (2008). *Teaching for student learning: Becoming a master teacher*. Boston: Houghton Mifflin.

Schunk, D.H. (1987). Peer models and children's behavioral change. *Review of Educational Research*, 57, pp. 149–74.

Schunk, D.H. (2000). *Learning theories: An educational perspective*, 3rd ed., Columbus, OH: Merrill/Prentice Hall.

Schunk, D. H., & Hanson, A. R. (1985). Peer models: Influences on children's self-efficiency and achievement. *Journal of Educational Psychology*, 77, pp. 313–22.

Schwartz, B., & Reisberg, D. (1991). *Learning and memory*. New York: Norton.

Slavin, R. (1994). *Educational psychology*, 5th ed. Boston: Allyn & Bacon.

Soar, R. S. (1973). *Follow-through classroom process measurement and pupil growth: Final report*. Gainesville, FL: Institute for Development of Human Resources, College of Education, University of Florida.

Solomon, D., & Kendall, A. J. (1976). *Individual characteristics and children's performance in varied educational settings*. Rockville, MD: Montgomery County Public Schools.

Taba, H. (1967). *Teacher's handbook for elementary school social studies.* Reading, MA: Addison Wesley.

Wolvin, A. D. (1983). Improving listening skills. In R. B. Rubin (ed.). *Improving speaking and listening skills: New directions for college learning assistance,* no. 12. San Francisco: Jossey-Bass.

PART III

Barrows, H. S., & Myers, A. C. (1997). *Problem-based learning: A total approach to education.* Monograph from Problem-Based Learning, H. S. Barrows & A. C. Kelson (eds.), Alexandria, VA: Association for Supervision and Curriculum Development.

Bloom, B. S. (1976). *Human characteristics and school learning.* New York: McGraw-Hill.

Bloom, B. S. (1968). *Learning for mastery.* Evaluation Comment, 1(2). Los Angeles: University of California, Center for the Study of Evaluation of Instructional Programs.

Blumenfeld, P., Soloway, E., Marx, R., Krajcik, J., Gudzial, M., & Palinscar, A. (1991). Motivating project-based learning: Sustaining the doing, supporting the learning. *Educational Psychologist,* 26(3 & 4), 369–98.

Bruner, J. (1961a). *The process of education.* Cambridge, MA: Harvard University Press.

Bruner, J. (1961b, Winter). Act of discovery. *Harvard Educational Review,* 31(1), 21–32.

Carroll, J. B. (1963). A model of school learning. *Teachers College Record,* 64, 722–33.

Cohen, E. G. (1994). *Designing groupwork: Strategies for the heterogeneous classroom* (2nd ed.). New York: Teachers College Press.

Dewey, J. (1938). *Experience and education.* New York: Collier.

Dewey, J. (1916). *Democracy and education.* New York: Macmillan.

Fertman, C., White, G., & White, L. (1996). *Service learning in the middle school: Building a culture of service.* Columbus, OH: National Middle School Association.

Fuchs, L. S., Fuchs, D., Hamlett, C. L., & Karns, K. (1998). High achieving students' interactions and performance on complex mathematical tasks as a function of homogeneous and heterogeneous pairings. *American Educational Research Journal,* 35, 227–68.

Gunter, M. A., Estes, T. H., & Schwab, J. (1999). *Instruction: A models approach,* 3rd ed. Boston: Allyn & Bacon.

Hunter, R. (2004). *Madeline Hunter's mastery teaching: Increasing instructional effectiveness in elementary and secondary schools*, Updated edition. Thousand Oaks, CA: Corwin Press.

Hutchings, P., & Wurtzdorff, A. (1988). Experiential learning across the curriculum: Assumptions and principles. In P. Hutchings & A. Wurtzdorff (eds.), *New Directions for Teaching and Learning*, no. 35. San Francisco: Jossey-Bass.

Jensen, E. (1998). *Teaching with the brain in mind*. Alexandria, VA: Association for Supervision and Curriculum Development.

Johnson, D. W., & Johnson, R. T. (1999). *Learning together and alone: Cooperation, competition, and individualization* (5th ed.). Boston: Allyn & Bacon.

Johnson, D. W., & Johnson, R. T. (1994). *Learning together and alone: Cooperation, competition, and individualization* (4th ed.). Boston: Allyn & Bacon.

Johnson, D. W., & Johnson, R. T. (1991). *Learning together and alone*. Englewood Cliffs, NJ: Prentice-Hall.

Jones, B. F., Rasmussen, C. M., & Moffitt, M. C. (1997). *Real-life problem solving: A collaborative approach to interdisciplinary learning*. Washington, DC: American Psychological Association.

Joyce, B., Weil, M., with Calhoun, E. (2004). *Models of teaching*, 7th ed. Boston: Pearson.

Kendall, J. C. & Associates (eds.) (1990). *Combining service and learning: A public resource book for community and public service*. 2 vols. Raleigh, NC: National Society for Internships and Experiential Education.

Kottler, J. A., & Kottler, E. (2000). *Counseling skills for teachers*. Thousand Oaks, CA: Corwin Press.

Krajcik, J. S., Czemiak, C., & Berger, C. (1999). *Teaching children science: A project-based approach*. Boston: McGraw-Hill.

Krajcik, J. S., Blumenfeld, P., Marx, R., & Soloway, E. (1994). A collaborative model for helping middle grade science teachers learn project-based instruction. *Elementary School Journal*, 94, 483–97.

Leighton, M. S. (2006). Cooperative learning. In J. M. Cooper Ed., *Classroom teaching skills*, 8th ed., pp. 273–312. Boston: Houghton Mifflin.

McLester, S. (2011, March). *Learning gets personal.* www.districtadministration.com.

Michaelis, J. U. (1963). *Social studies for children in a democracy*. Englewood Cliffs, NJ: Prentice-Hall.

Piaget, J. (1952). *The origins of intelligence in children*. New York: Basic Books.

Piaget, J. (1954). *The construction of reality in the child* (M. Cook, trans.). New York: Basic Books.

REFERENCES

Resnick, L. B. (1987). *Education and learning to think*. Washington, DC: Academic Press.

Robinson, A., & Clinkenbeard, P. R. (1998). Giftedness: An exceptionality examined. In J. T. Spence, J. M. Darley, & D. J. Foss (eds.), *Annual Review of Psychology* (pp. 117–39). Palo Alto, CA: Annual Reviews.

Sharan, S. (1990). Cooperative learning and helping behavior in the multiethnic classroom. In H. C. Foot, M. J. Morgan, & R. H. Shute (eds.). *Children helping children* (pp. 151–76). New York: J. Wiley & Sons.

Sharan, Y., & Sharan, S. (1992). *Group investigation: Expanding cooperative learning*. New York: Teachers College Press.

Slavin, R. E. (1995). *Cooperative learning: Theory, research, and practice*, 2nd ed., Boston: Allyn & Bacon.

Slavin, R. E., Karweit, N. L., & Wasik, B. A. (eds.) (1994). *Preventing early school failure: Research, policy and practice*. Boston: Allyn & Bacon.

Slavin, R. E. (1987). Ability grouping and student achievement: A best-evidence synthesis. *Review of Educational Research*, 57, 293–336.

Staudt. C. (2005). *Changing how we teach and learn with handheld computers*. Thousand Oaks, CA: Corwin Press.

Stepien, W., Johnson, T., & Checkley, K. (1997). *Problem-based learning, Facilitator's guide*. Alexandria, VA: Association for Supervision and Curriculum Development.

Thelen, H. (1960). *Education and the human quest*. New York: Harper and Row.

Vygotsky, L. S. (1978). *Mind in society: The development of higher mental process*. Cambridge, MA: Harvard University Press.

ABOUT THE AUTHOR

Marie Pagliaro is a professional development consultant. She was full professor and director of the Teacher Education Division at Dominican College; chair of the Education Department at Marymount College; supervisor of student teachers at Lehman College of the City University of New York; and chair of the Science Department and teacher of chemistry, general science, and mathematics in the Yonkers Public Schools. She received her Ph.D in Curriculum and Teaching from Fordham University.

www.ingramcontent.com/pod-product-compliance
Lightning Source LLC
Chambersburg PA
CBHW021215240426
43672CB00026B/325